A Student's Guide to

ROBERT
FROST

Titles in the **UNDERSTANDING LITERATURE** *Series:*

A Student's Guide to
EMILY DICKINSON
0-7660-2285-4

A Student's Guide to
F. SCOTT FITZGERALD
0-7660-2202-1

A Student's Guide to
NATHANIEL HAWTHORNE
0-7660-2283-8

A Student's Guide to
ERNEST HEMINGWAY
0-7660-2431-8

A Student's Guide to
ARTHUR MILLER
0-7660-2432-6

A Student's Guide to
WILLIAM SHAKESPEARE
0-7660-2284-6

A Student's Guide to
JOHN STEINBECK
0-7660-2259-5

UNDERSTANDING
LITERATURE

A Student's Guide to

ROBERT
FROST

Connie Ann Kirk, Ph.D.

Enslow Publishers, Inc.

40 Industrial Road   PO Box 38
Box 398   Aldershot
Berkeley Heights, NJ 07922   Hants GU12 6BP
USA   UK
http://www.enslow.com

Library of Congress Cataloging-in-Publication Data

Kirk, Connie Ann.
    A student's guide to Robert Frost / by Connie Ann Kirk.— 1st ed.
        p. cm. — (Understanding literature)
    Includes bibliographical references and index.
    ISBN 0-7660-2434-2
    1. Frost, Robert, 1874-1963—Juvenile literature. 2. Poets, American—20th
century—Biography—Juvenile literature. I. Title. II. Series.
    PS3511.R94Z7619 2005
    811'.52—dc22

                                        2005013392

Printed in the United States of America

10 9 8 7 6 5 4 3 2 1

To Our Readers:
We have done our best to make sure all Internet Addresses in this book were active
and appropriate when we went to press. However, the author and the publisher
have no control over and assume no liability for the material available on those
Internet sites or on other Web sites they may link to. Any comments or suggestions
can be sent by e-mail to comments@enslow.com or to the address on the back cover.

Illustration Credits: AP/Wide World Photos, pp. 17, 136; Getty Images,
pp. 15, 107, 118, 121, 125, 129, 133; Library of Congress, pp. 12, 49, 114,
138; Robert Frost Collection (#6261), Clifton Waller Barrett Library of
American Literature, Special Collections, University of Virginia Library,
pp. 26, 44, 57, 93, 110.

Cover Illustration: Library of Congress (inset); Corel Corporation/Hemera
Technologies, Inc. (background objects).

✦· Dedication ·✦

*To Mum
with childhood memories of
January 20, 1961*

CONTENTS

FROM FARMER POET TO POET LAUREATE

The Life and Times of Robert Frost

His father died when he was only eleven years old. He was co-valedictorian of his high school class, an honor he shared with a bright girl whom he later convinced to marry him. He was a poultry farmer and he grew apples. He was a teacher of first grade through college. He was a father of six, but only four of his children—three daughters and one son—lived into adulthood. He lived to be eighty-eight years old. All of these things would make a full life for any man, but for Robert Frost, these details tell only part of the story. In addition to all of these things, Robert Frost was a poet.

His poems were so well regarded that he won the Pulitzer Prize for Poetry an unprecedented four times, and he became Consultant in Poetry at the

Library of Congress, a position later called Poet Laureate of the United States. His titles, like "The Road Not Taken" and "Stopping by Woods on a Snowy Evening," rank among the most popular and widely recognized American poems ever written. He won the Bollingen Prize for Poetry and was given forty-four honorary doctorate degrees from universities all across the United States, England, and Ireland.

Ironically, Robert Lee Frost, who is most associated with rural New England, was named after the famous Confederate general of the Civil War and spent his earliest years near the ocean in the city of San Francisco. Unlike Robert E. Lee, Robert Frost's battles were not waged with weapons against the Union but instead were wrought with words against inner enemies like the difficult emotions of loss and loneliness that afflict everyone.

As an old man, the poet delivered one of his poems, "The Gift Outright," at the inauguration of President John F. Kennedy in 1961. Robert Frost, farmer-poet, who was born nine years after the end of the Civil War and four years after the death of his famous namesake, became one of the most celebrated American poets of the twentieth century.

Who was this New England poet who came from

Robert E. Lee—*General Robert E. Lee (1807-1870) was the conflicted Virginia military officer who became general of the Confederacy rather than fight against his family for the Union. Much beloved in the South and respected in the North, Lee won important victories for the Confederacy. Lee's surrender to General Ulysses S. Grant of the Union Army at Appomattox Courthouse, Maryland, ended the Civil War. Interestingly, after the war, Lee's application papers for reinstating his U.S. citizenship were misplaced. It was not until the 1970s that President Jimmy Carter, a Georgian whose last name Lee's mother shared, officially pardoned Lee of all misdeeds against the United States.*

San Francisco? What qualities of his poems still make them so popular and well-regarded today?

COMMON SUBJECTS AND TECHNIQUES

Robert Frost's poems are often set in rural New Hampshire, Vermont, and Massachusetts, where he spent the majority of his adult life. This is one reason he has been called a New England poet. Many of his poems paint vivid pictures of the New England countryside, including such common scenes as pastures and meadows, apple and birch trees, old barns, and stone walls. His poems offer a departure from an older kind of poetry known as pastoral. In pastoral poems, the poet expresses a longing for the simplicity of rural

This photo of Robert Frost was taken circa 1915, at about the age of forty-one.

life over the complexity of urban life. In pastoral poems, the poet believes that nature offers food for the soul, or spiritual comfort and enlightenment that it is not possible to obtain from any aspect of living in the city.

Frost's poems do reveal a preference for the countryside in their speakers, or narrators; however, nature in a Frost poem does not always offer the full comfort the speaker seeks. If the natural landscape does provide some rest from the struggles of life, it is often only for a brief moment. Rural life presents its own kind of challenges, terrors, and even tragedies. Nevertheless, Frost's poems show that if any ease from emotional or spiritual conflict is to be found anywhere, the countryside offers more possibilities than anywhere else.

Frost regarded intonation, the natural rise and fall in pitch of voices engaged in informal speech, as a sound that he wanted to capture in his poetry. He called this quality "the sound of sense," reflecting the idea that intonation carries meaning in conversation just as the words themselves do. He said that one can almost follow a conversation taking place behind a closed door by listening carefully to the intonation of the speakers' voices, without hearing the actual words. Frost sought to

INTONATION—*The natural rise and fall in pitch of human voices engaged in informal speech.*

13

METER—*A regular pattern of stressed and unstressed syllables in poetry.*

put this sound into his poetry. This may be one reason why so many readers have found his work easier to understand than the work of some other poets. It may also be a reason why his poems flow so naturally when read aloud.

MODERNISM—*A movement in literature and art that began in the early twentieth century.*

While he uses "the sound of sense" in his poems, Frost resists the trend of other poets of his day to break out of the use of formal, fixed structures of meter and rhyme. Unlike the modernist poets such as Ezra Pound, who wrote in free verse, Frost stayed within the traditional forms of regular meter and exact rhyme. He said, "I had as soon write free verse as to

FREE VERSE— *Poetry that does not follow a traditional fixed form. Instead, the poet allows the form of the poem to rise "organically" out of the subject matter of the poem.*

play tennis with the net down."[1] This showed that he regarded the limitations of writing within poetic forms as a necessary tool of writing good poetry. Frost's preference for traditional forms makes his poetry seem old-fashioned to some readers today, but the poet did not care about that. He was writing poetry that made the most sense to him in the way that he wanted to write it. He said,

Frost pets a calf while relaxing on his farm in Vermont in January 1942.

EXACT RHYME—*When two or more words end with the same vowel and consonant sounds. It is the traditional rhyme most people think of, for example:* wall *and* ball.

"My object is true form—is was and always will be—form true to any chance bit of true life."[2]

Frost wrote about loss and loneliness, the beauty of nature, the struggle to make decisions and concern over making the wrong one, getting along with one's neighbors, and many other subjects. Though he wrote about the change of seasons and small occurrences that may seem at first to have little importance in the grand scheme of things, the themes of his poetry have universal appeal. Frost uses the everyday events of rural New England life as metaphors for thinking about the larger questions of what it means to be a human being alive anywhere in the world.

Frost wrote different kinds of poetry, but he is most known for his lyric and narrative poems. The word lyric comes from the Old French word "lyre," which was a stringed musical instrument in the Middle Ages. Troubadours in France used to walk the countryside, singing and playing original songs on their lyres in exchange for food and lodging. Today, song "lyrics" refer to the words of a song and the melody refers to its music. Lyric poetry has a musical quality, and the poems are normally personal and

Seventy-year-old Robert Frost sits behind a desk in his Cambridge home in March 1945.

METAPHOR—*A comparison between two seemingly unlike things without using the words "like" or "as," for example:* All the world is a stage.

emotional. Lyric poetry uses imagery, frequently engaging more than one of the five senses; lyric poems are typically shorter poems. Examples of lyric poems by Robert Frost include "After Apple-Picking" and "The Road Less Traveled."

In contrast to lyric poems, narrative or dramatic poems tell a story. In dramatic poetry, the poet allows the *personae* or characters in the poem to act out the story, and there may be dialogue in the poem. Examples of Frost's narrative poems include "The Death of the Hired Man" and "Mending Wall."

DRAMATIC POEM—*Verse that tells a story through action and dialogue, as though it were a miniature play.*

READING POETRY

Reading poetry is a different kind of exercise than reading a newspaper or a chapter in a textbook. It uses different skills. Below are some tips that help readers gain more from the experience of reading poetry:

1. Read the poem more than once.
2. Read the poem aloud. When experienced poetry readers read aloud, they do not stop at

the end of every line. Instead, they follow the punctuation. So, if there is no period at the end of a line, readers do not stop there. Instead, they continue through to the next line or even the next until they reach the end of the sentence, wherever that may be in the poem. When you get used to following the punctuation, soon you begin to hear the "music" of the poem as you read. If possible, it helps to hear a recording or live performance of the poet reading the poem; however, this should not be necessary to enjoy a poem.

3. Look up vocabulary you do not understand. Consider different definitions for the same word. Also try to find out when the poem was written (the date is often supplied with the poem). Think about how language changes over time. Could this word have had a different meaning a long time ago than it does today?

4. Stay open to different interpretations that strike you as you read and reread the poem. It helps to remember that a poem is never "about" any one thing, just like a painting is never "about" only one thing. A good poet is not trying to convey a specific, hidden message in poetic code that you have to decipher. If you look at a painting, you see different aspects of it—composition,

line, shapes, colors, subjects, brush strokes, facial expressions, background details, and so forth. These features make you think of different things, and you take different thoughts away from the painting. You also may form an overall impression from looking at it.

Poetry is similar. Think of rereading a poem as standing to the side of, backing away from, or moving closer to a painting. Sometimes changing your view by rereading a poem shifts the meaning of the words in your mind. Let new thoughts come in and challenge old thoughts. It is the variety of these thoughts—not the struggle to find some single, magic "right" answer to a puzzle—that poetry is "about."

5. Realize that it is possible to interpret poems in many ways. Think of a favorite song—the song will bring up one set of memories for one person and perhaps an entirely different set for someone else. One person may think the song is happy and another thinks it is sad or melancholy. Similarly, the images in the poem will bring different thoughts to each reader.

While poems have different interpretations, it is possible to misread poetry. You cannot put into a poem what is not there. In other words, when you say a poem suggests a theme of enjoyment of the outdoors to you, you must be able to point to evidence inside the poem that supports your interpretation. Your reading must "work" for every line. If even one line does not seem to support your view, then your interpretation needs more thought and effort. It might help to interpret (find meaning in) the poem if you explicate, or reword each line of, the poem.

6. Finally, be prepared to not understand a poem on an intellectual or logical level to your complete satisfaction. Sometimes, the sensory qualities—the sounds of the words or the visual imagery the poem brings to mind—are enough, whether or not you think you "understand" what the poem may be "about," or think you have "figured out" what you think the poet is "trying to say." Many poets could not even give you the definitive explanation you might seek. Poetry is art, and art sometimes really does not "mean" anything as much as it simply exists as a new human creation.

EXPLICATE—
To explain each line of a poem in your own words.

* * *

Frost's poems are still read, recited, and studied in schools and universities in the early twenty-first century. Recently, Frost's poems have been regarded as a bit old-fashioned because of their heavy use of rhyme and poetic forms. More modern poets have favored free verse that is less formal and has fewer rhymes. Even so, many of Frost's poems remain among the all-time favorites of American citizens and readers around the world. Capturing the passionate emotions represented in "the sound of sense" within the traditional forms of poetry, Frost believed he was working to find a way to put some kind of order on the confusion human beings so often encounter by living in the world. He called the art form of poetry "a momentary stay against confusion."[3]

A SWINGER OF BIRCHES

Early to Middle Years, 1874–1912

There was a rough edge to Frost's personality and poetry that people understand better if they know a bit about his background, especially his early years. Though his ancestral roots are in New England and Ohio, Robert Frost was born in San Francisco, California, on March 26, 1874.

A POET'S PARENTS

According to Jay Parini's *Robert Frost: A Life*, William Prescott Frost, Jr., the poet's father, was a Harvard graduate who worked as a journalist and dabbled in politics. He was named city editor of the San Francisco *Daily Evening Post* and ran unsuccessfully for the Democratic candidacy for his district's Congressional seat in 1882. In 1884, he ran for, but lost, a position as city tax collector.

Will Frost was also a drinker and a ruffian. He kept a pistol and a jar of pickled bull's testicles on his desk to warn people not to bother him. He chewed tobacco and made regular use of the brass spittoon he kept behind his desk. Will's father was a millworker who had tried to rein in his son with little success. Will ran away from New England to join the Confederate army under Robert E. Lee, only to be swiftly caught and brought home again. He later went West to try to cure his thirst for adventure, much as the gold prospectors did. The poet's father liked to walk the streets of San Francisco to release some of his pent-up energy. Taking frequent walks was a trait his son would carry with him back East.

The poet's mother, Belle (Isabelle) Moodie, was born in Leith, Scotland, and spoke with a lilting Scottish brogue all of her life. Her father died at sea when she was eight years old, and three years later her mother sent her to live in Ohio with a well-off aunt and uncle. Belle grew up religious and bookish. She met Will Frost at Lewistown Academy in Pennsylvania, where both worked as teachers. Though they were quite opposite in temperament, they shared interests in literature and thought. Belle initially refused Will's proposal of marriage, saying that she preferred to dedicate her life to teaching and would never marry. However, the couple eventually married on March 18, 1873.

EARLY MEMORIES

Some of the poet's earliest memories revolved around his father. He remembered taking long walks with him along the ocean shore, and standing fearfully alone on the beach watching his father swim in San Francisco Bay. He recalled distinctly when his father, sporting an important-looking frock coat and top hat, boarded a train to travel east as a delegate to the Democratic convention in Cincinnati in 1882. His father chaired the Democratic committee for San Francisco in 1884, and "Robbie," as Robert Frost was called when he was little, remembered being carried through town in a victory ride on top of a fire engine when Grover Cleveland won the presidency.

His father's political ambitions were not rewarded, however. Will Frost went on a drinking binge when he lost his bid to be city tax collector. He was difficult to live with and much of the time he was ill or drunk or both. He took to hanging out at the Bohemian Club with his journalist and artist friends rather than stay home and be involved with his family. He also liked to gamble, an avocation his family could not afford. Worse, he could be violent. One afternoon he came home drunk and saw Robbie and his friends building a boat from wood they found in an open lot. Will Frost was so angry at the sight of

Robert Frost as a baby.

the glue and sticks spread around that he stepped on the half-built ship and hit Robbie several times with the back of his hand.

Belle Frost tried to cope with the downturn in her family life by clinging to the church. She began to study and practice a denomination of Christianity established by the eighteenth-century mystic Emanuel Swedenborg. The Swedenborg doctrine had a complex system of beliefs that were embraced by writers such as Ralph Waldo Emerson. Belle also believed she had second sight and could predict the future. Though he did not become a regular church-goer, young Robbie did pick up on his mother's sense of knowing things that went beyond what was visible. As early as age seven, he reported hearing voices and being clairvoyant, and these were beliefs his mother encouraged.

When she was pregnant again, Belle took Robbie away from the abusive environment around his father and went east to live with Will's parents. Her baby, Jeanie Florence Frost, was born on June 25, 1876, in Lawrence, Massachusetts. Though the couple reconciled enough for Belle to take the children back to California for a time, the family would soon have to deal with Will's bad habits again as well as his declining health.

BETTER TIMES

Young Robbie enjoyed weekend outings in California as pleasant as Belle could make them. They went to Woodward's Gardens where the future poet enjoyed the botanical displays and aquatic merry-go-round. They also took long walks around the city, especially up Telegraph Hill, Russian Hill, and Nob Hill. Robbie liked the mansions atop Nob Hill and enjoyed the views of the ocean below provided by all of the climbs. Belle Frost read to her children from books such as *Tom Brown's School Days*, by Thomas Hughes, and *The Last of the Mohicans*, by James Fenimore Cooper. She also read to them from Scottish authors such as the poet Robert Burns and some works she wrote herself, such as her published story *The Land of Crystal*, or, *Christmas Days with the Fairies*.

Occasionally Will would join his wife and children when they went to picnics sponsored by the Caledonian Club, a Scottish group through which Belle kept up her ancestral ties. At the picnics, the adults would be entertained by traditional Celtic music, and the children took part in foot races. Will was a walker and runner, so he was pleased to watch Robbie excel at running. He bought him a pair of running shoes one year to encourage his son's athleticism. Robert was an exceptional athlete all through school.

FATHER'S ILLNESS

Despite his tough persona, Will Frost was a sick man. In addition to his alcoholism, he developed tuberculosis. He started coughing up blood, and the outlook for his future was grim. His strong personality kept him plunging forward, trying to find a cure. At one point, he tried a folk remedy that involved going to a slaughterhouse and drinking several cups of blood taken from a steer's freshly cut throat.

Since he had let his life insurance policy lapse, Will wrote home to his parents in Massachusetts to ask them to take care of his family when he died. He worked up until the day before his death, on May 5, 1885. He left his wife and children with only $8.00 in the bank after his funeral expenses were paid—a small amount of money, even in those days.

MOVE TO NEW ENGLAND

Though Belle Frost resisted going to her in-laws for help, she had few alternatives after the death of her husband. Will had asked to be buried in his family's plot back in New England, so she and the children, at her in-law's expense, needed to accompany his coffin on the train all the way across the country from

California to Massachusetts. Though they took their daughter-in-law and grandchildren in, the elder Frosts were cool towards them to say the least. Grandfather Frost had a long white beard and small wire-rimmed glasses. He did not appreciate this upheaval in his comfortable Yankee life. He held a prominent place in the mill town of Lawrence. Grandmother Frost was high-strung and nervous. Belle Frost's mystical religious beliefs and progressive methods of children-rearing struck her as strange and foreign.

It was in this household and with his father's relatives that Robert Frost had his first prolonged exposure to life in New England. Soon, his mother began taking various teaching jobs around the area to try to support herself and her children. She found a job teaching fifth grade in Salem, New Hampshire, and she took the children to live with her there in a small apartment. Robbie's Aunt Sarah, his father's sister, lived on a farm in Amherst, New Hampshire. Her husband, Ben Messer, known to the children as Uncle Messer, felt sorry for his nephew and niece and encouraged them to visit the farm. There, they escaped the small apartment in Salem and played in the pastures and barns, on the dirt roads, and along the stone walls in the wide-open New England countryside.

"BIRCHES"

It was at Messer's farm that the young Robert Frost began to connect with the aspects of New England country life that would be the hallmark of his poems. At this time, he engaged in a boyhood country pastime called swinging birches. In 1886, his fearless new best friend, Charley Peabody, also 12 years old at the time, taught him how to do it, climbing the narrow, white-barked trees until they gave way and bent to the ground. The "swinger" landed on his feet as the trunk bowed to the ground under his weight.

One of Frost's best known poems is titled "Birches."

* * *

"BIRCHES"

When I see birches bend to left and right
Across the lines of straighter darker trees,
I like to think some boy's been swinging them.
But swinging doesn't bend them down to stay
As ice storms do. Often you must have seen them
Loaded with ice a sunny winter morning
After a rain. They click upon themselves
As the breeze rises, and turn many-colored
As the stir cracks and crazes their enamel.
Soon the sun's warmth makes them shed
   crystal shells
Shattering and avalanching on the snow-crust—
Such heaps of broken glass to sweep away

You'd think the inner dome of heaven had fallen.
They are dragged to the withered bracken by
   the load,
And they seem not to break; though once they
   are bowed
So low for long, they never right themselves:
You may see their trunks arching in the woods
Years afterwards, trailing their leaves on the ground
Like girls on hands and knees that throw their hair
Before them over their heads to dry in the sun.
But I was going to say when Truth broke in
With all her matter-of-fact about the ice storm,
I should prefer to have some boy bend them
As he went out and in to fetch the cows—
Some boy too far from town to learn baseball,
Whose only play was what he found himself,
Summer or winter, and could play alone.
One by one he subdued his father's trees
By riding them down over and over again
Until he took the stiffness out of them,
And not one but hung limp, not one was left
For him to conquer. He learned all there was
To learn about not launching out too soon
And so not carrying the tree away
Clear to the ground. He always kept his poise
To the top branches, climbing carefully
With the same pains you use to fill a cup
Up to the brim, and even above the brim.
Then he flung outward, feet first, with a swish,
Kicking his way down through the air to the ground.
So was I once myself a swinger of birches.

And so I dream of going back to be.
It's when I'm weary of considerations,
And life is too much like a pathless wood
Where your face burns and tickles with cobwebs
Broken across it, and one eye is weeping
From a twig's having lashed across it open.
I'd like to get away from earth awhile
And then come back to it and begin over.
May no fate willfully misunderstand me
And half grant what I wish and snatch me away
Not to return. Earth's the right place for love:
I don't know where it's likely to go better. I'd like
to go by climbing a birch tree,
And climb black branches up a snow-white trunk
Toward heaven, till the tree could bear no more,
But dipped its top and set me down again.
That would be good both going and
    coming back.
One could do worse than be a swinger of birches.

* * *

In the poem, the speaker reminisces about a fun activity from his boyhood. First he compares the bent-over birches he sees in the woods as the result of an ice storm to the trees bent over from children swinging on them. He would rather the ones he sees in adulthood that "click upon themselves" full of ice be instead bent over by bearing a boy's weight from his playing on them. As the icy trees of "Truth" leave the speaker's attention, he allows himself to dream about his past and imagine a boy riding his father's trees to the ground, subduing them, conquering them, one by one. The poem moves in more closely to reveal that the speaker himself is the boy. He admits to wishing he could go back to those days when he was a swinger of birches, going up and down, up and down.

The poem is not limited to nostalgia for the past, however. Frost uses imagery to visually and aurally compare ice storm birches to the swinging birches. He uses simile to compare the fallen birches to girls drying their flung-over hair in the sun. Through metaphor, he compares life to a "pathless wood." He describes climbing the tree as going toward heaven and

SIMILE—*A comparison between two seemingly unlike things using the words "like" or "as," for example:* My love is **like** a red, red rose.

swinging down the tree as falling back to earth in order to begin again on another tree, repeating the process over and over. The climb and fall back to earth involve fear and daring, safety and resurrection. The act of swinging birches mimics new growth and death in Nature. Trees themselves grow toward the sky and drop their leaves each autumn only to have them grow back again in the spring. By saying that one could do worse than swing on birches, Frost may be implying that one can take comfort in being part of the cycle of Nature.

Look closely at the persona of the boy in the poem. Notice that he is swinging on his father's birches, and that he does this as a way of playing alone, since he lives too far from town to learn to play baseball. Knowing what you do so far about Frost's biography, how do these two traits compare and contrast with Frost's own life as a boy? Why might this boy want to "subdue" and "conquer" his father's birches until he "took the stiffness out of them?" What, besides life, might birch trees symbolize in the poem?

SCHOOLING A POET

Robert Frost was a quick learner who did well in school. Like his father before him, he played and enjoyed competitive sports, including baseball and, later, football. In baseball he excelled as a pitcher. He developed a fastball that he called a "jump ball," as well as a curve ball and a drop ball. When he was twelve, his dream was to become a major league pitcher. He would go on to talk knowledgeably about the game and its statistics into old age, and he played whenever he had the chance from his youth on into middle age.

In high school, Robert studied Latin and Greek on the college preparatory track at Lawrence High School, his father's alma mater. He joined the Debate Society, played on the varsity football team as a tight end, and also played tennis. Frost became friends with Carl Burell, who was in his mid-twenties. He had come back to finish high school after spending years working at jobs to support himself.

Burell had a thirst for books and knowledge. He was interested in botany, especially, and also in writing. Frost looked up to him as an adult authority figure who was not as stern as his grandfather. Burell encouraged Frost's early attempts at writing and at observing nature. When Burell contributed some of his writing to the high school *Bulletin*, Frost also sent in a poem, "La Noche Triste," which became his first publication. The school paper also published "Song of the Wave." Both poems were published in Frost's sophomore year.

By his senior year, Frost expected to graduate at the top of his class and go to Harvard. There were two wrinkles that upset this plan. The first was that he tied for valedictorian with Elinor Miriam White. She had drawn his attention by more than her brilliance in the classroom—young Frost also found his rival attractive. The second factor that changed his plans was that his father's parents did not approve of Harvard as a choice for their grandson's college education. Will Frost had gone there and had come away with a drinking problem. The Frosts maintained that Harvard was a "drinking school." One of Frost's teachers had graduated from Dartmouth in Hanover, New Hampshire. As a second choice, Frost enrolled there after he won a scholarship that would pay most of his tuition. His grandparents paid for his room and board.

DARTMOUTH DAYS

Dartmouth College was founded in 1769 by a Congregational minister from Connecticut named Reverend Eleazar Wheelock. The Royal Governor of New Hampshire, John Wentworth, allocated the land for the college and helped secure its charter from King George III. The charter established an institution "for the education and instruction of the Youth of the Indian tribes in this land . . . and also of English Youth and any others."[1] The school is named after a supporter of Wheelock's, William Legge, who was the Second Earl of Dartmouth. The Ivy League school is the ninth-oldest college established in the United States and is the last institution of higher learning in the nation to be founded under British colonial rule.

The summer before college, Frost and Elinor White became secretly engaged. White went to St. Lawrence University in Canton, New York, and Frost went on his way to Dartmouth. They wrote letters back and forth. Elinor enjoyed college life. When he arrived in Hanover, New Hampshire, Frost missed

Elinor but tried to fit in with college life and devote himself to his studies and to writing.

Right away, he found that college life, for him, left much to be desired. He had already read much of the material being presented in his classes. Looking back on his Dartmouth days later in life, he said, "I'm afraid I wasn't much of a college man . . . I was getting past the point where I could show any great interest in any task not self-imposed."[2] Neither did he fancy the social life of fraternities and other organizations on campus. He later reflected, "I was invited into a fraternity—Theta Delta Chi—and joined up . . . One of my 'rich' classmates paid my initiation fee. But somehow I was no fraternity brother."[3]

Frost began taking walks alone along the Connecticut River, going north, or he took a carriage to the town of Etna then hiked up the mountain trails from there. Often, he left his room in Wentworth Hall at night simply to take a walk in the woods by himself. When his fraternity brothers became concerned and went looking for him, they asked him what he did while spending so much time in the woods. "I gnaw bark," was his reply.[4] Ironically, Frost would return many years later to teach in the very same building where he once lived on campus as a student. Dartmouth would eventually contain the largest collection of Frost manuscripts and papers in the world.

One of the two most significant literary effects on Frost during his student days at Dartmouth was his purchase in the bookstore of *Palgrave's Golden Treasury of Songs and Lyrics,* edited by Francis Palgrave. This book was an anthology of poetry that Frost read over and over again and cherished all of his life. The book contained hundreds of lyrics by British poets as well as a detailed explanation of poetry that influenced many poets of the time in England and the United States.

Palgrave wrote that lyric poetry "turn[s] on some single thought, feeling, or situation" and that it "gives treasure 'more golden than gold,' leading us in higher and healthier ways than those of the world, and interpreting to us the lessons of Nature."[5] One testament to Frost's admiration for *Palgrave's Golden Treasury* is that he used it in his classroom years later when he was a teacher, asking students to memorize twenty poems from it as part of their assignments. The anthology, in fact, was valued the world over and has not been out of print since it was first published in 1860.

The second major impact of Frost's time at Dartmouth also occurred outside the classroom. Once, while in the library, Frost spotted a journal called *The Independent* that had published a poem by a poet from Dartmouth. The poem and editorial about it took up the entire front page. The poem was "Seaward: An Elegy on the Death of Thomas William Parson," by Richard Hovey. Frost later claimed that this was the first time it occurred to him to send his poetry to a national publication which would pay to publish it. Soon, he wrote his own elegy and sent it off to the magazine—"My Butterfly: An Elegy." When *The Independent* published the poem on November 8, 1894, it became Robert Frost's first national publication.

STANZA—*A grouping of poetic lines separated by a space.*

* * *

"MY BUTTERFLY"
(first stanza)
Thine emulous fond flowers are dead, too,
And the daft sun-assaulter, he
That frighted thee so oft, is fled or dead:
Save only me
(Nor is it sad to thee!)—
Save only me
There is none left to mourn
    thee in the fields.

* * *

Frost became disillusioned with college and dropped out at the end of December 1892. He did not like being told what to read and when to read it and believed that if one knew how to read, one did not

"My Butterfly"

> As his first nationally published poem, "My Butterfly" now stands as a work uncharacteristic of Frost's style. Instead of using the natural, informal speech of rural New Englanders for which he would become famous, in this poem, Frost later admitted, "I was . . . guilty of 'theeing' and 'thouing,' a crime I have not committed since."[6]

need much formal instruction beyond that. Perhaps some of his philosophy of education came from his mother and her efforts at homeschooling.

In fact, it was to his mother's aid that he first went when he arrived home. Belle Frost had continued to teach and was having a difficult time with a particularly disrespectful and unruly class of adolescents. Frost went to the Methuen school board and asked them to allow him to substitute for her at the Second Grammar School. The board agreed. Frost's strategy of classroom management would be one that would land him in jail today, though it was not unusual at the time. He went to the local hardware store and bought a rattan cane and used the threat of it to enforce the behavior he expected from his students. The school board was pleased with the improvement in student behavior, saying that Frost showed "maturity" in handling a difficult situation. For his part, the experience was enough to cement in Frost the desire to write poetry for a living. He was well aware, however, that one could not survive on poetry alone.

Not long after this, Frost took a job at the Arlington Woolen Mill in Lawrence, Massachusetts, as a light trimmer. He worked in the dynamo room, changing carbon filaments in ceiling lamp bulbs. The job involved climbing tall ladders over the tops of machinery and reaching up at awkward angles, often with no leverage. The danger of falling was great. When work was slow, the poet often climbed out on the roof of the factory and read Shakespeare.

Frost often talked about his experience working in the mill when he wanted to comment with authority on what it was like to work hard for a living. While he was a millworker, he also wrote occasional pieces for the Lawrence *Daily American* and the *Sentinel*, like his father before him. But unlike for his father, journalism would not be his calling.

In 1894, Frost quit the mill and began working as a schoolteacher in Salem, New Hampshire. The situation was better than his first experience with the disruptive class, and the pay was equal to what he was getting at the mill, but the hours were shorter. He could devote more of his free time to writing the poetry that he loved.

After the publication of "My Butterfly" in *The Independent*, Frost began corresponding extensively with the editor, Susan Hayes Ward, about literature and writing. Their many letters back and forth show that Ward and her brother, William Hayes Ward, another editor at the journal, believed they had discovered a promising poet and wanted to encourage him. Letters from Frost to the Wards show a poet thinking and articulating his views about poetry in a serious and thoughtful way. His letters show a growing confidence in his ideas. The correspondence and friendship with the Wards, especially Susan, would last nearly four decades.

Meanwhile, after some time at home to help care for her ailing sister, Elinor White continued her college education at St. Lawrence, despite Frost's urgings that she come home to stay and marry him. She was much more pleased with college life than he anticipated and showed no sign of homesickness. She refused to marry him unless and until he had steady employment. No doubt, the desire to marry motivated Frost to stay gainfully employed in teaching and writing.

Marriage, Fatherhood, and Harvard

Robert Frost and Elinor White married on December 19, 1895. On September 25, 1896, the couple's first child, Elliot, was born. Frost went back and forth

Robert Frost's wife, Elinor.

TWILIGHT

One of the ploys Frost used to convince Elinor to marry him was to collect five of his original poems into a special edition dedicated to her that he titled Twilight. *He paid to have only two copies of the book, one for each of them, printed on antique paper and had it bound in pebbled brown leather. When he arrived at St. Lawrence University to hand-deliver Elinor her copy and explain to her what he had done in order to impress her, he found that he had arrived outside of the strict hours that the college allowed men to visit women. Elinor quickly took the book from him and, without allowing him to explain, told him to take the next train home. Severely disappointed, Frost destroyed his companion copy of the book. Not long afterwards, he took a trip south to fight off his frustration, visiting an area along the Virginia-North Carolina border called the Dismal Swamp. Elinor's valuable copy of* Twilight *is now housed at the University of Virginia.*

between teaching and helping his mother establish a school and working as a reporter. With a new and growing family, Frost again attempted college in order to secure a more stable income. He passed the entrance exams for Harvard in 1897. That fall, he moved his wife, son, and mother-in-law to Cambridge where he began his studies.

The poet's father left a legacy at Harvard University. At what his parents later called a "drinking school," Will Frost had received the Bowditch Scholarship and was the winner of the Bowdoin Prize and other awards for his academic achievements. He was elected to Phi Beta Kappa and gave an address at

Commencement to his fellow classmates of the class of 1872.

The journalist's son went to Harvard under very different conditions. He was already twenty-three years old, married, and a father. In addition to his studies, he had to take a job off campus to help with expenses. He did this by serving as principal of the Shepard Evening School in North Cambridge. His mother still needed his help in Salem, and Elinor was pregnant with their second child.

Frost found his studies of the classics at Harvard exhilarating, but the cost in terms of his personal life became too great. When illness struck a number of his family members, the balance Frost tried hard to maintain among job, school, and family fell apart. In the spring of 1899, his second year at Harvard, he withdrew from the college in good standing. Lesley, the couple's first daughter, was born on April 28, 1899.

DERRY FARM

Once again, Grandfather Frost came to Robert Frost's aid. The patriarch purchased a farm on the Londonderry Turnpike at Derry, New Hampshire, for $1,725. He allowed the young Frost family to live on the farm and work. They made an arrangement that if the poet would farm there for a decade, his grandfather would hand over the deed to the property. The family took over the 30-acre farm in 1900 and set it up for poultry farming. The Derry farm provided economic stability to Robert Frost and his young family just at the time when they needed it most.

The year they moved into the farmhouse and began working the land, however, was a tough one. The summer before the move, Frost's son, Elliot, died of cholera. Belle Frost, the poet's devoted and troubled mother, died of cancer a few months later. Frost's grandfather died the following year, and his will left the Derry farm and a share of an annuity to Frost.

More children arrived while the Frost family lived on the farm. A son named Carol was born on May 27, 1902; Irma was born on June 27, 1903; and Marjorie was born on March 28, 1905. Another daughter, Elinor Bettina, was born on June 18, 1907, but she lived only three days.

Daily life at the farm involved taking out or bringing in the cow or harnessing Eunice, the horse, for a ride into town or to work in the pasture. Walks were common forms of entertainment. Elinor worked in the kitchen at a soapstone sink and helped gather the daily round of eggs. Robert tended to the land, livestock, buildings, and fences. He also worked on his poems in the parlor on a writing board that lay across the arms of an easy chair.

Frost and Elinor both taught their young children at home and encouraged their efforts at observation and creative projects. Years later, daughter Lesley's journals were published in *New Hampshire's Child*, and the notebooks and creations of the Frost siblings were written about in a 1994 book by Frost's granddaughter, Lesley Lee Francis. The book is called *The Frost Family's Adventure in Poetry: Sheer Morning Gladness at the Brim*.

The first few years at Derry farm provided a brief moment in time when Frost was isolated in the country with his family and was free to observe everything around him and to write and think. It is as if the farm was the incubator of Frost's creativity and became the source and means of his outstanding work. The family lived at Derry Farm for ten years. Frost family roots grew so deep into the soil that the farm later came to be called the Derry Homestead among the family and is now called the Robert Frost Farm.

Even in the early 1900s, however, Frost could not earn enough money from farming alone to support a family of four children. As a consequence, for the latter half of the decade, he also taught at Pinkerton Academy in nearby Derry Village. By 1909, the family moved into Derry Village to be closer to the school. When the administration of the school shifted personnel, the principal moved on to Plymouth

Normal School in Plymouth, New Hampshire. He invited Frost to come along.

Frost, whose reputation as a teacher had grown statewide after his years at Pinkerton, decided to sell the Derry Farm and move to Plymouth. Derry Farm had made its permanent mark on him, however, creating an impact that would be part of his life and

Robert Frost on the front steps of the Pinkerton Academy in Derry, New Hampshire, circa 1910.

work the rest of his days. Frost wrote about the lasting impact of Derry Farm in a 1952 letter:

> You might be interested to know that during my ten years in Derry the first five of them farming altogether and the last five mostly teaching but still farming a little, I wrote more than half of my first book much more than half of my second and even quite a little of my third, though they were not published till later. I might say the core of all my writing was probably the five free years I had there on the farm . . . The only thing we had plenty of was time and seclusion. I couldn't have figured on it in advance. I hadn't that kind of foresight. But it turned out as right as a doctor's prescription.[7]

Derry Farm's importance to American literature was reinforced years later when the property was rescued by the State of New Hampshire. Over the years, Frost had occasionally wanted to regain family ownership of the farm but for one reason or another had never done so. The property lay deteriorating and had turned into an auto graveyard. Hundreds of old cars and tires were piled up on the grounds; the buildings lay in severe disrepair. When the State of New Hampshire purchased the farm, the land was cleared, and the house and barn restored. The farm was named a National Historic Landmark in 1977.

OFF TO ENGLAND

By 1912, it became clear to Frost that the poems he wrote or began at Derry Farm were significantly better in quality than anything he had written before. The time had come to take a chance and pursue his dream of preparing his poems for publication. So far, he had only had a few poems published in small journals. He had always dreamed of putting together a collection of poems in a book. Selling his grandfather's house and interests gave him enough money to take his family away from New England for awhile. The family began considering where they might go so that Frost could complete his book. Frost first thought of Vancouver, British Columbia, but Elinor dreamed of a place where they could live under a thatched roof. Eventually, they settled on England. They particularly wanted to find a cottage in the countryside, somewhere not far from London.

On August 23, 1912, Robert, Elinor, and their surviving children (Lesley, 13; Carol, 10; Irma, 9; and Marjorie, 7) boarded the steamship *Parisian* to cross the ocean to England and unknown adventures. Nothing was certain except that Robert Frost was going to leave New England to focus on writing and publishing poems.

CHAPTER 3

"MENDING WALL"

Frost in England, 1912–1915

Robert Frost lived in England for more than two years, from September 1912 through February 1915. In that time, he soaked up the literary landscape of British poets and playwrights, met such poets as American Ezra Pound and Irishman William Butler Yeats, and completed two collections of poems. His first book was *A Boy's Will*, published in England in 1913. The second was *North of Boston*, published there in 1915. Later, both books would also be published in the United States.

The family settled in a rented cottage called The Bungalow that was not unlike their farmhouse in Derry. It was located in Beaconsfield, Buckinghamshire, about twenty miles north of London. Frost wrote most mornings and often worked until late afternoon. Elinor taught the two younger children at home and helped her husband edit and order the poems for his collections. Frost looked over the poems he had brought with him that he had written while teaching and farming. He discarded some and held onto others and eventually worked to develop a theme for a book. The theme was about a young boy who moves from solitude to fellowship, from being afraid of life to embracing life through love. He added one or two new poems, and then he approached a publisher.

The manuscript was not only accepted for publication by David Nutt and Company, but the publisher also wanted first rights to look at the manuscripts for his next four books as well, whether they were poetry or prose. *A Boy's Will* was published in England just seven months after the Frosts arrived in the country. The book did not receive rave reviews, but it did capture the attention of Ezra Pound, who wrote about the poet's promise in the United States as part of a piece denouncing American editors. Frost would not forget this kindness from Pound years later, when Pound himself needed support.

"Mowing"

Frost's favorite poem from *A Boy's Will* was "Mowing." It is an example of a pastoral poem. Most likely, Frost wrote the poem while still living in Derry, New Hampshire. It is probably one that he brought with him across the Atlantic Ocean to England to work into his first book. The poem is one of the early examples of Frost trying to create poems that sounded like everyday speech put into strict formal lines, or what he called "talk song." A mower swings a scythe back and forth across a field, cutting grass for hay. A scythe is a farming tool with a long blade at the end of a handle.

* * *

"MOWING"

There never was a sound beside the wood but one,
And that was my long scythe whispering to
   the ground.
What was it it whispered? I knew not well myself;
Perhaps it was something about the heat of the sun,
Something, perhaps, about the lack of sound—
And that was why it whispered and did not speak.
It was no dream of the gift of idle hours,
Or easy gold at the hand of fay or elf:
Anything more than the truth would have seemed
   too weak
To the earnest love that laid the swale in rows,
Not without feeble-pointed spikes of flowers
(Pale orchises), and scared a bright green snake.
The fact is the sweetest dream that labor knows.
My long scythe whispered and left the hay to make.

* * *

Frost employs imagery in creating the scythe and its swishing or whispering sound as the mower swings it back and forth. He also uses personification with the scythe, giving it human characteristics. The speaker of the poem thinks back to mowing, remembers the swishing sound, and wonders what the scythe may have been whispering about as it worked. Perhaps it was whispering something about how hot the sun was, the mower thinks, or how it

> **PERSONIFICATION—**
> *A poetic device in which inanimate objects and animals are given human characteristics, for example:* The flower sipped the raindrops.

was so quiet there in the countryside that the scythe thought it needed to whisper.

Line 13, about fact being the best dream that work knows, became one of Frost's favorite lines. He said that line comes as close as he ever got to a definition of poetry. In writing "Mowing," Frost began to learn that his own brand of art lay in the small details of everyday life and in thinking closely about commonplace objects, like the scythe. The scythe cuts the grass, but it does not make hay. The hay is made later in the hot sun. The grass is cut in rows by the mower, just as the poet puts down lines of words. The poet, like the mower, can only create the lines. Like cut grass drying to become hay over time, the words must be picked up line by line and made into a poem later on by the reader.

***

In early 1914, the Frost family moved to another cottage called Little Iddens in Dymock,

Gloucestershire. There, Frost became familiar with a group of poets known as the Dymock poets. These included the writers Lascalles Abercromie, Rupert Brooke, and Edward Thomas. Later that year, the family moved to a farmhouse in Ryton called The Gallows. Frost continued to write, take long walks around the English countryside, and visit with poets and friends.

Frost's second collection, *North of Boston*, was published by David Nutt and Company the same year. This book was the breakthrough book for Robert Frost and his poetry. It received good reviews in England and was later picked up by an American publisher, Henry Holt and Company, which went on to publish most of Frost's future collections of poems.

Like the majority of poems Frost brought with him from the United States that make up *A Boy's Will*, the sixteen poems in *North of Boston* were composed primarily in New England. The distance of space and time seemed to ignite a burst of creative energy in the poet. He broke through the more traditional techniques he used in *A Boy's Will* and tried new things. One technique was his "sound of sense" method of inserting the natural voice of New England speech into lines of fixed forms. Rather than focus inward on the self as *A Boy's Will* does, *North of Boston* considers the lives of other everyday New Englanders who live in the countryside. The collection contains several of the poems for which

Frost's cottage home Little Iddens, where the family
lived beginning in 1914.

Frost is still most revered today—poems such as "Mending Wall," "The Death of the Hired Man," and "After Apple-Picking."

"MENDING WALL"

Frost uses dramatic monologue in this poem. The speaker describes a conversation he had with his neighbor while mending a stone wall that ran the border between their two properties.

> **Dramatic Monologue**—A dramatic monologue is a complex kind of poetic technique first attributed to the English poet Robert Browning. It is a poem in which the speaker tells the poem to a listener inside the poem. This internal listener is called the auditor. The reader "eavesdrops" on what is being said and, therefore, has the advantage of distance to make judgments about both the speaker and the auditor.

* * *

"MENDING WALL"

Something there is that doesn't love a wall,
That sends the frozen-ground-swell under it,
And spills the upper boulders in the sun,
And makes gaps even two can pass abreast.
The work of hunters is another thing:
I have come after them and made repair
Where they have left not one stone on a stone,
But they would have the rabbit out of hiding,

To please the yelping dogs. The gaps I mean,
No one has seen them made or heard them made,
But at spring mending-time we find them there.
I let my neighbor know beyond the hill;
And on a day we meet to walk the line
And set the wall between us once again.
We keep the wall between us as we go.
To each the boulders that have fallen to each.
And some are loaves and some so nearly balls
We have to use a spell to make them balance:
"Stay where you are until our backs are turned!"
We wear our fingers rough with handling them.
Oh, just another kind of outdoor game,
One on a side. It comes to little more:
There where it is we do not need the wall:
He is all pine and I am apple orchard.
My apple trees will never get across
And eat the cones under his pines, I tell him.
He only says, "Good fences make good neighbors."

* * *

Each spring the stone wall needs mending after stones fall off or out of it during the winter. As the two neighbors walk along on either side of the wall mending it together, the speaker comments to his neighbor that there is something about walls that people really do not like. Walls can be offensive to those being walled in or walled out, he says. In a way, all walls are meant to be taken down and even seem at times to crumble on their own. The farmer on the other side of the wall, however, repeats a saying he learned from his father, that walls are good things; they make good neighbors. He does not have any bad feelings towards his neighbor. He simply thinks the wall keeps things clear and orderly for both of them.

By setting up these two views of walls, taken from both "sides" of the issue, as it were, Frost has "built" a metaphor that readers may interpret in many ways. One interpretation of the poem is that the poem speaks to the American struggle between the right of every individual to live in freedom without limitation versus the practical need for all citizens to have their lives, loved ones, and belongings protected.

In interviews, Frost said that he was as much a builder as a destroyer of walls. He said he gave equal time to both farmers in the poem, using repetition of both of their key lines. The farmer who likes walls appears to be inspired by Frost's own neighbor in Derry, New Hampshire, who did have pine trees along his side of a stone wall as is expressed in the poem. Even so, Frost maintained that he could be the farmer walking along either side of the wall.

Close to the end of his life, the poet was sent on a goodwill mission to the Soviet Union to meet with Premier Nikita Khrushchev during the Cold War. While in Moscow, he recited "Mending Wall." Few people who heard it then could avoid thinking of the divide between the Soviet Union and the United States, symbolized by the Berlin Wall separating the West from the East in Germany.

"The Death of the Hired Man"

In addition to "Mending Wall," "The Death of the Hired Man" was another poem from *North of Boston* that received especially close attention and praise. It depicts a married farming couple, Mary and Warren, who are revisited by Silas, a man they had hired previously to help around the farm. Silas proved not to be a reliable hired man and left the couple during haying time the year before, just when they needed him most. This is a long dramatic poem, something like a story told through action and dialogue, as though it were a miniature play. Years later, this poem was even produced as a play.

* * *

"DEATH OF THE HIRED MAN"

Mary sat musing on the lamp-flame at the table,
Waiting for Warren. When she heard his step,
She ran on tiptoe down the darkened passage
To meet him in the doorway with the news
And put him on his guard. "Silas is back."
She pushed him outward with her through the door
And shut it after her. "Be kind," she said.

She took the market things from Warren's arms
And set them on the porch, then drew him down
To sit beside her on the wooden steps.

"When was I ever anything but kind to him?
But I'll not have the fellow back," he said.
"I told him so last haying, didn't I?
If he left then, I said, that ended it.
What good is he? Who else will harbor him
At his age for the little he can do?
What help he is there's no depending on.
Off he goes always when I need him most.
He thinks he ought to earn a little pay,
Enough at least to buy tobacco with,
So he won't have to beg and be beholden.
'All right,' I say, 'I can't afford to pay
Any fixed wages, though I wish I could.'
'Someone else can.' 'Then someone else will
    have to.'
I shouldn't mind his bettering himself
If that was what it was. You can be certain,
When he begins like that, there's someone at him
Trying to coax him off with pocket money—
In haying time, when any help is scarce.
In winter he comes back to us. I'm done."

"Sh! Not so loud: he'll hear you," Mary said.

"I want him to: he'll have to soon or late."
"He's worn out. He's asleep beside the stove.
When I came up from Rowe's I found him here,
Huddled against the barn door fast asleep,
A miserable sight, and frightening, too—

You needn't smile—I didn't recognize him—
I wasn't looking for him—and he's changed.
Wait till you see."

        "Where did you say he'd been?"

"He didn't say. I dragged him to the house,
And gave him tea and tried to make him smoke.
I tried to make him talk about his travels.
Nothing would do: he just kept nodding off."

"What did he say? Did he say anything?"

"But little."

        "Anything? Mary, confess
He said he'd come to ditch the meadow for me."

"Warren!"

        "But did he? I just want to know."

"Of course he did. What would you have him say?
Surely you wouldn't grudge the poor old man
Some humble way to save his self-respect.
He added, if you really care to know,
He meant to clear the upper pasture, too.
That sounds like something you have heard before?
Warren, I wish you could have heard the way
He jumbled everything. I stopped to look
Two or three times—he made me feel so queer—
To see if he was talking in his sleep.
He ran on Harold Wilson—you remember—
The boy you had in haying four years since.
He's finished school, and teaching in his college.
Silas declares you'll have to get him back.

He says they two will make a team for work:
Between them they will lay this farm as smooth!
The way he mixed that in with other things.
He thinks young Wilson a likely lad, though daft
On education—you know how they fought
All through July under the blazing sun,
Silas up on the cart to build the load,
Harold along beside to pitch it on."

"Yes, I took care to keep well out of earshot."

"Well, those days trouble Silas like a dream.
You wouldn't think they would. How some
   things linger!
Harold's young college-boy's assurance piqued him.
After so many years he still keeps finding
Good arguments he sees he might have used.
I sympathize. I know just how it feels
To think of the right thing to say too late.
Harold's associated in his mind with Latin.
He asked me what I thought of Harold's saying
He studied Latin, like the violin,
Because he liked it—that an argument!
He said he couldn't make the boy believe
He could find water with a hazel prong—
Which showed how much good school had
   ever done him.
He wanted to go over that. But most of all
He thinks if he could have another chance
To teach him how to build a load of hay—"

"I know, that's Silas' one accomplishment.
He bundles every forkful in its place,

And tags and numbers it for future reference,
So he can find and easily dislodge it
In the unloading. Silas does that well.
He takes it out in bunches like big birds' nests.
You never see him standing on the hay
He's trying to lift, straining to lift himself."

"He thinks if he could teach him that, he'd be
Some good perhaps to someone in the world.
He hates to see a boy the fool of books.
Poor Silas, so concerned for other folk,
And nothing to look backward to with pride,
And nothing to look forward to with hope,
So now and never any different."

Part of a moon was falling down the west,
Dragging the whole sky with it to the hills.
Its light poured softly in her lap. She saw it
And spread her apron to it. She put out her hand
Among the harplike morning-glory strings,
Taut with the dew from garden bed to eaves,
As if she played unheard some tenderness
That wrought on him beside her in the night.
"Warren" she said, "he has come home to die."
You needn't be afraid he'll leave you this time."

"Home," he mocked gently.

                    "Yes, what else but home?
It all depends on what you mean by home.
Of course he's nothing to us, any more
Than was the hound that came a stranger to us
Out of the woods, worn out upon the trail."

"Home is the place where, when you have to
  go there,
They have to take you in."

                    "I should have called it
Something you somehow haven't to deserve."

Warren leaned out and took a step or two,
Picked up a little stick, and brought it back
And broke it in his hand and tossed it by.
"Silas has better claim on us you think
Than on his brother? Thirteen little miles
As the road winds would bring him to his door.
Silas has walked that far no doubt today.
Why doesn't he go there? His brother's rich,
A somebody—director in the bank."

"He never told us that."

                    "We know it, though."

"I think his brother ought to help, of course.
I'll see to that if there is need. I ought of right
To take him in, and might be willing to—
He may be better than appearances.
But have some pity on Silas. Do you think
If he had any pride in claiming kin
Or anything he looked for from his brother,
He'd keep so still about him all this time?"

"I wonder what's between them."

                    "I can tell you.
Silas is what he is—we wouldn't mind him—
But just the kind that kinsfolk can't abide.

He never did a thing so very bad.
He don't know why he isn't quite as good
As anybody. Worthless though he is,
He won't be made ashamed to please his brother."

"*I* can't think Si ever hurt anyone."

"No, but he hurt my heart the way he lay
And rolled his old head on that sharp-edged
    chair-back.
He wouldn't let me put him on the lounge.
You must go in and see what you can do.
I made the bed up for him there tonight.
You'll be surprised at him—how much
    he's broken.
His working days are done; I'm sure of it."

"I'd not be in a hurry to say that."

"I haven't been. Go, look, see for yourself.
But, Warren, please remember how it is:
He's come to help you ditch the meadow.
He has a plan. You mustn't laugh at him.
He may not speak of it, and then he may.
I'll sit and see if that small sailing cloud
Will hit or miss the moon."

                            It hit the moon.
Then there were three there, making a dim row,
The moon, the little silver cloud, and she.

Warren returned—too soon, it seemed to her—
Slipped to her side, caught up her hand and waited.

"Warren?" she questioned.

                    "Dead," was all he answered.

Nearly the entire poem is expressed through the conversation of Mary and Warren. Mary tells Warren in hushed tones that she found Silas lying asleep and unwell against the barn door. She took him inside the house and gave him some tea, trying to get him to talk about where he had been since he left them. Mary says that Silas was confused, but he talked to her about wanting to work for them again. Silas claimed that he and Harold Wilson, a younger hand who had also worked at the couples' farm, would be good partners and will get a lot of work done around the farm this season.

Harold Wilson had worked for Mary and Warren four years before, but he had since graduated from college and begun teaching. Silas told Mary he remembered arguing with Wilson about the value of education when they had worked together. Wilson studied Latin, but Silas knew how to build a perfect load of hay. Silas thinks Wilson needs to learn his trade of haying and that this will keep him from being a "fool of books."

The conversation between Mary and Warren continues throughout the poem as Mary asks her husband to keep his voice low so as not to disturb Silas or to allow him to hear their talk. Mary tries to convince Warren to allow Silas to stay, to hire him for another season. She says that he has come "home" to die, that he will not run off again.

Warren does not want to rehire Silas because he is unreliable. He wants to know why Silas should come to them and not to his rich, banker brother's home thirteen miles away to die. Mary feels merciful toward Silas and shows Warren how the man has come to them out of pride and avoids his brother's house out of embarrassment. He is offering to work in order to keep his dignity intact as he dies. Finally, Warren agrees to go back in the house and see Silas, while Mary waits outside watching the moon. When Warren returns, however, he takes Mary's hand and he tells her that Silas has died.

Frost's description of home in the poem has become well-known—home is a place where, when you have to go there, the people there have to take you in. It is also a place where you can go even without deserving it. Mary and Warren have worked hard to establish a stable and caring home for themselves, but Silas has drifted from job to job, never settling down. When it comes time to die, Silas has nowhere to go, nowhere to really call home, except the couple's farm. Home, and all it represents—security, love, heaven, family, identity, fulfillment—all are out of reach for the hired man, unless the couple who supported him before take him in once more. They finally agree to do so, but by that time it is too late.

Looking biographically at the poem, one might

sense that its descriptions of home echo Frost's experience when his grandparents took in his family after his father died, even though it was against their wishes. Frost related to the hired man as well as with the farm couple. When a theatrical group dramatized this poem portraying the married couple as country hicks, Frost stormed backstage afterwards and angrily told the performers and producers how mistaken they were in their interpretation. The couple was educated, he said. They were both sensitive and intelligent people. Frost himself had both hired men to work on his and Elinor's farm as well as been a hired man when he was younger, doing haying and other chores around farms in New England. His old friend from high school, the well-read Carl Burell, also worked for the Frosts for a time as a hired man.

The title of the poem is a bit misleading, since the poem is not as much about the man who dies as it is about the couple discussing him. In his initial refusal to rehire Silas based on his past performance, Warren can be seen to represent justice, law, and responsibility. Mary is compassionate and forgiving toward Silas. She instinctively knows what is happening by his reappearing on their doorstep in such a feeble and worn-out condition. The poem dramatizes the love between the husband and wife who discuss what they should do about this turn of events. Mary's understanding of human nature and her explanation of it to her husband echoes conversations held between husbands and wives every day. When Warren takes her hand at the end of the poem, he expresses an understanding of her emotions, and the couple unites in their feelings toward Silas, even as Silas's soul escapes like the little silver cloud touching the moon.

Whispering Motif—*A motif is a pattern of images that reappears frequently throughout a poet's work. Notice how whispering and talking softly are a part of "Death of the Hired Man" as well as "Mowing." What does this recurring image of whispering in Frost's poetry suggest to you about rural life?*

"AFTER APPLE-PICKING"

The speaker of "After Apple-Picking" looks back and remembers the past, the days of apple-picking. What makes the poem more than simply a memory well told, however, is the way the poem seems to dwell in the state between memory and dream. The reader is uncertain whether the story of picking apples is factual or has been dreamed up by the speaker, or is some combination of the two.

"AFTER APPLE-PICKING"

My long two-pointed ladder's sticking
   through a tree
Toward heaven still,
And there's a barrel that I didn't fill
Beside it, and there may be two or three
Apples I didn't pick upon some bough.
But I am done with apple-picking now.
Essence of winter sleep is on the night,
The scent of apples: I am drowsing off.
I cannot rub the strangeness from my sight
I got from looking through a pane of glass
I skimmed this morning from the drinking trough
And held against the world of hoary grass.
It melted, and I let it fall and break.
But I was well
Upon my way to sleep before it fell,
And I could tell
What form my dreaming was about to take.
Magnified apples appear and disappear,
Stem end and blossom end,
And every fleck of russet showing clear.
My instep arch not only keeps the ache,
It keeps the pressure of a ladder-round.
I feel the ladder sway as the boughs bend.
And I keep hearing from the cellar bin
The rumbling sound
Of load on load of apples coming in.
For I have had too much
Of apple-picking: I am overtired.
Of the great harvest I myself desired.

There were ten thousand thousand fruit to touch,
Cherish in hand, lift down, and not let fall.
For all
That struck the earth,
No matter if not bruised or spiked with stubble,
Went surely to the cider-apple heap
As of no worth.
One can see what will trouble
This sleep of mine, whatever sleep it is.
Were he not gone,
The woodchuck could say whether it's like his
Long sleep, as I describe its coming on,
Or just some human sleep.

* * *

Critics have often pointed to allusions in "After Apple-Picking" that refer to the work of Ralph Waldo Emerson, the nineteenth-century essayist, poet, and philosopher. Frost was influenced early and lifelong by Emerson's writing and thought, particularly through

> **ALLUSION**—*A direct or indirect reference in a literary work to details from another literary work, mythology, history, or some other source.*

his mother's and Emerson's common affinity for the teachings of Emanuel Swedenborg. In an essay titled, "On Emerson," Frost called him "the poet" and one of the "four greatest Americans."[1]

The imagery of the ladder and the dream may be references to Emerson's essay, "Experience":

73

We wake and find ourselves on a stair: there are stairs below us, which we seem to have ascended; there are stairs above us, many a one, which go upward and out of sight . . . We have learned that we do not see directly, but mediately, and that we have no means of correcting these colored and distorting lenses that we are.[2]

The apple-picker's ladder could be an allusion to Emerson's stairs of experience. The ice from the drinking trough in the poem may be an allusion to Emerson's lens. It is at the moment when the speaker looks through the icy "pane of glass" in the poem that the poem appears to drift off into a dreamworld and away from memory. Frost once described the poem as containing "the intoxication of extreme exhaustion."[3] Perhaps the distortion Emerson writes of when looking at one's experience is reflected in the extreme fatigue of the speaker in Frost's poem.

At the point in the poem where the speaker looks through the icy pane and seems to go into a dream state, the imagery remains just as clear as if the speaker was remembering his days in the orchard. He can still feel the pressure of the ladder rung on the arches of his feet; see the sight of the apple blossoms and stems; and hear the sound of apples tumbling into bins. He is long tired now, though, of picking apples. He no longer desires the "great harvest" of "ten thousand thousand fruit." The speaker

Ralph Waldo Emerson—*Emerson was born in Boston in 1803 and was educated at Harvard. He was ordained as a Unitarian minister in 1829 but became disillusioned with the church at the untimely death of his first wife. After some time in England, Emerson became a lecturer and essayist back in the United States and was attracted to the teachings and mysticism of Emanuel Swedenborg. A group of thinkers, poets, and others, such as Anson Alcott (father of the writer Louisa May Alcott) and Henry David Thoreau, worked with Emerson to establish a new American identity in literature and art. Their belief system, which involved a spiritual connection between human beings and Nature, was called "Transcendentalism." These artists and their work became part of a rich cultural era in the mid-1800s known as the "American Renaissance." Emerson died in 1882 when Robert Frost was still a child living in California.*

acknowledges that what will bother him in his sleep, if sleep it is, are the apples that he dropped, the ones that surely went to the cider mill. no matter if they were bruised or not.

Many readers are somewhat startled and confused by the appearance of the woodchuck at the end of a poem that seems to be about picking apples. Some critics believe the image is another allusion to Emerson. He states in his essay "Nature" from *Essays: Second Series* (1844), "let us be men instead of woodchucks."[4] In Emerson's essay "Fate," he also describes hibernation as the "long sleep."[5] In saying the speaker would have asked the woodchuck about the "long sleep" were he not already gone, Frost may be making a tongue-in-cheek reference to Emerson himself.

The speaker seems to wonder if his long sleep is hibernation, like the woodchuck's, and he will return another day to work and forage for food, or whether it is a human sleep, which could mean death or some other kind of inactivity or lack of attentiveness.

Different interpretations of "After Apple-Picking" abound. The apple-picking may be seen to represent any kind of labor from which one has grown tired, or perhaps it is a metaphor for the general rigors of living everyday life. Readers have also associated apples in the poem, and particularly apples falling to the ground, with Adam and Eve and their fall from grace in the Bible's Book of *Genesis*.

Labor Motif—*Notice how many of Frost's poems contain personae or characters who are farmers or other kinds of workers or that portray work in progress. How does this motif express the American way of life?*

* * *

The Frosts decided to leave England a bit earlier than they had originally planned because of World War I, which began in Europe in the summer of 1914. Their journey back across the Atlantic Ocean was fearful for all of them in February 1915. In addition to the seasickness that plagued many members of the Frost family, all passengers of the ship, *St. Paul*, also had to sleep in their bunks fully clothed and wearing life jackets. The threat of German attacks on passenger ships at the time was very real. As the ship churned through rough waters, Robert Frost is said to have wondered what he would find when he reached home in his beloved New England. He was concerned that he may have left his greatest success behind him in England and that Americans might not embrace his work and new ideas about poetry. Still, he knew that one American publisher was already going to print his poems. It was time to see what would happen to his career in his homeland, which was, after all, the source and subject of most of his work.

"THE ROAD NOT TAKEN"

The Return to New England, 1915–1920

When the Frost family returned to the United States in 1915, the poet sent his wife and four children ahead of him "north of Boston" while he took care of some business affairs in the city. Much to his surprise, reviews of *North of Boston* by influential American critics and poets such as Ezra Pound and Amy Lowell had propelled his name as a poet to watch into the national spotlight. Editors wanted to meet with him; universities and other organizations wanted him to come and speak or read his poems; movers and shakers in the literary world wanted to meet him in person and discuss plans, ideas, and projects.

Within a few months of the family's arrival back in

the country, Henry Holt and Company had published both *A Boy's Will* and *North of Boston* in American editions. Ironically, the twentieth-century poet who would become so linked with a uniquely American kind of poetry was actually "discovered" in England. Ezra Pound noted this fact in his writing and endured some criticism for it from American editors. After he returned from that first trip to England, Robert Frost, now already into his early 40s, became a permanent fixture on the American poetry scene.

FRANCONIA

Frost knew that he could write better when he farmed than when he taught school. That summer, the family settled on a farm in Franconia, New Hampshire, and the poet resumed listening to the everyday rural people he encountered to gather new material for poems. Rather than lead a quiet farm life as he had in the past, however, now Frost was contacted frequently to give lectures or readings or meet with members of the literary establishment.

"OUT, OUT—"

Though this poem is based on a real incident that happened in Bethlehem, New Hampshire, in 1910, Frost did not write this poem until 1915 when he was living in Franconia. It became part of his first collection published after his return to the United States. The collection was called *Mountain Interval* and was published in 1916. The poem first appeared in *McClure's Magazine* in July 1916. Because of the tragedy it portrays about a young person, Frost refused to recite it as part of his public readings.

* * *

"OUT, OUT—"

The buzz-saw snarled and rattled in the yard
And made dust and dropped stove-length sticks
   of wood,
Sweet-scented stuff when the breeze drew across it.
And from there those that lifted eyes could count
Five mountain ranges one behind the other
Under the sunset far into Vermont.
And the saw snarled and rattled, snarled
   and rattled,
As it ran light, or had to bear a load.
And nothing happened: day was all but done.
Call it a day, I wish they might have said
To please the boy by giving him the half hour
That a boy counts so much when saved from work.
His sister stood beside them in her apron
To tell them "Supper." At the word, the saw,
As if to prove saws knew what supper meant,
Leaped out at the boy's hand, or seemed to leap—
He must have given the hand. However it was,
Neither refused the meeting. But the hand!

80

The boy's first outcry was a rueful laugh,
As he swung toward them holding up the hand,
Half in appeal, but half as if to keep
The life from spilling. Then the boy saw all—
Since he was old enough to know, big boy
Doing a man's work, though a child at heart—
He saw all spoiled. "Don't let him cut my hand off—
The doctor, when he comes. Don't let him, sister!"
So. But the hand was gone already.
The doctor put him in the dark of ether.
He lay and puffed his lips out with his breath.
And then—the watcher at his pulse took fright.
No one believed. They listened at his heart.
Little—less—nothing!—and that ended it.
No more to build on there. And they, since they
Were not the one dead, turned to their affairs.

* * *

The incident on which the poem is based was described in a newspaper article in the *Littleton Courier*. The story involved a 16-year-old boy, Raymond Tracy Fitzgerald, one of the twin sons of Michael G. and Margaret Fitzgerald of Bethlehem, New Hampshire. The boy was helping saw wood outside when he accidentally hit the loose pulley which caused the saw to come down on his hand, nearly cutting it off. Suffering from shock, Raymond was taken into the house, and a doctor was summoned right away. Unfortunately, Raymond died quickly afterward, from heart failure due to shock. Frost and his children had met the Fitzgeralds during the summer when they visited Bethlehem.

The poem's title is an allusion to Shakespeare's famous lines from *Macbeth*:

> Out, out, brief candle!
> Life's but a walking shadow, a poor player
> That struts and frets his hour upon the stage,
> And then is heard no more; it is a tale
> Told by an idiot, full of sound and fury,
> Signifying nothing.[1]

The title is the first clue that the poem is about a life cut short, in this case, quite literally. In the play, Macbeth is mourning the death of his wife. The title suggests that the life of a farm boy has every bit as much nobility as the life of a king or queen.

The narrative poem has an objective tone nearly like the newspaper article where the story first appeared. The boy has been working all day with no event. Imagery of the smell and sight of the sawdust and the sound of the saw that "snarled and rattled" make the poem come alive. The five Vermont mountain ranges remain stately in the distance beneath the setting sun. It has been a long day of work. The boy apparently wished to knock off work a half hour early so that he might enjoy a short bit of the day, but that was not to be. Instead, he keeps working until his sister comes out of the house to call them in for supper.

At the surprise of her words over the sound of the saw, according to the speaker of the poem, the saw "leaped out" for the boy's hand, nearly cutting it off.

The boy's first response is to laugh; however, it is a laugh of terror. Then his life flashes before his eyes, and he imagines what life would be like for a man without a hand as a farmer in New England. As an adolescent, he has a child's heart living inside a man's body, and he cries out for his sister not to let the doctor cut off his hand. His hand is already gone, however, and the boy slips into unconsciousness. The one watching over him at his bedside suddenly notices there is no pulse, and then his heart slowly beats to "Little—less—nothing!" The boy has died. Frost's conclusion to the poem stands in stark contrast to its anticipation of sentiment. Instead of showing a grieving family crying, Frost portrays the family going about their own affairs, since they were not the ones who died.

In one reading, the poem may be interpreted as a cautionary tale against industrialization, or the dangerous power of machines in conflict with nature. As the boy is working and the day goes by, the buzz saw is heard snarling and rattling in contrast to the views of the quiet rural countryside—the mountains and the sunset. When the buzz saw seems to hear the word "Supper" and "Leaped out at the boy's hand," the saw is *personified*; it seemingly comes alive to attack the boy. All is not well in rural life, Frost seems to be saying. In his twist on the genre of pastoral poetry, Frost shows that the country ought not be idealized; it can be a dangerous, tragic, and unforgiving place, just like the city or anywhere else.

After the boy dies, those who remain simply go about their affairs, which may possibly mean that they go back to work or prepare for another day of work tomorrow. One has to be dead in this world not to have work. Simple survival in the rural society of the poem depends on one's ability to work long and hard with one's hands. Some readers interpret the chilly ending of this poem as a negative comment on the Puritan work ethic of New England. Other readers see the ending as simply a truthful statement that honors the tragedy of the event and the family's grief by describing their initial response matter-of-factly, and not wrapping it in sentimentality, by overdramatizing it.

The collection in which this poem appeared, *Mountain Interval*, did not initially sell as well as *North of Boston*. The latter book sold 20,000 copies in its first year, which was an astounding number for a book of poetry. Still, its earnings were not enough to replenish Frost's savings after the long trip to England with his family. A reliable income was still something the father of four needed very much.

AMHERST COLLEGE

Alexander Meiklejohn, the president of Amherst College, and Stark Young, a popular professor there, invited Frost to come teach at the Massachusetts college for the spring semester of 1917. They offered him $2000 to teach two classes. One course would be a creative writing class in poetry that met only one evening a week, and the other was a larger class on English drama before Shakespeare.

Frost needed the money and liked the town of Amherst, which he had visited earlier when he gave a poetry reading at the college. It was, and still is, a small town in a rural area with a progressive intellectual community. Still, he knew that, for him, teaching and writing did not mix. The offer to keep his teaching load light with only two classes apparently sealed the deal. Once again, he moved his family, this time to a yellow wood-frame house on Dana Street, near campus. Robert and Elinor enrolled the children in local Amherst schools.

Frost enjoyed his poetry workshop with college students. The class met upstairs in the Beta Theta Pi fraternity house, which bordered the park-like Amherst Common. The students sat in worn leather chairs around a log fire listening to Frost discuss his theories of poetry, including "sound of sense." Often he read to them from the works of Amherst native Emily Dickinson, England's William Wordsworth, and others. Students brought the poems they were working on to the workshop, and Frost offered comments on their work. He was a generous teacher in these classes, often staying long after the end of class and inviting students back to his home for more discussion.

Students in the drama class were apparently less impressed with their instructor than were the budding poets. Frost often began class with whatever was on his mind that day, and he was very opinionated and did not hide his views. If he was unhappy about something to do with faculty or administration politics at Amherst College, he made this known. He gave no history or other background to the plays they were reading but instead focused only on the text.

He did not seem to care whether or not the students were interested in his lectures. Many of them played cards in the back of the room unnoticed. If students came to him seeking advice about dropping out of college to join the army and serve in the war, Frost encouraged them. He himself had dropped out of Dartmouth and Harvard and found nothing negative in doing so for almost any reason a young person might have. Frost had a disagreement with Stark Young that grew to such proportions that he asked the president of the college to fire him. When the president refused, Frost resigned.

Despite their prickly and controversial visiting author, the administration of Amherst College liked having Robert Frost on campus. They liked the notoriety that a nationally recognized poet who wrote about their native New England brought to the school. They would invite him back again and again, tempting him back to teaching with enticements like an honorary master of arts degree. Robert Frost would teach on and off at Amherst College for the rest of his life, including appointments in 1923–1925, 1926–1938, and 1949–1963. The college bestowed an honorary doctorate of letters on him in 1948.

"THE ROAD NOT TAKEN"

Mountain Interval included a poem that is arguably one of the best-known poems Robert Frost ever wrote. It is titled "The Road Not Taken."

* * *

"THE ROAD NOT TAKEN"

Two roads diverged in a yellow wood,
And sorry I could not travel both
And be one traveler, long I stood
And looked down one as far as I could
To where it bent in the undergrowth;

Then took the other, as just as fair,
And having perhaps the better claim,
Because it was grassy and wanted wear;
Though as for that, the passing there
Had worn them really about the same,

And both that morning equally lay
In leaves no step had trodden black.
Oh, I kept the first for another day!
Yet knowing how way leads on to way,
I doubted if I should ever come back.

I shall be telling this with a sigh
Somewhere ages and ages hence:
Two roads diverged in a wood, and I—
I took the one less traveled by,
And that has made all the difference.

* * *

While living in Derry, New Hampshire, Frost once wrote in a letter that he frequently came upon cross-roads on his walks in the countryside. He commented that it was curious to him that neither of the roads seemed well traveled.

In England, Frost and his friend, Edward Thomas, used to take walks together collecting rare plants. Even though the terrain was familiar to Thomas, he frequently had difficulty deciding which path to follow. Frost remarked on his habit that no matter which path he chose each time, he would always sigh and wonder about what might have been down the other path. Frost claimed that he began "The Road Not Taken" sitting on a couch in the middle of England, but he did not finish it there.

When Frost returned to New England, he received a letter from Edward Thomas who was trying to decide about joining the British forces to fight in World War I. Frost mailed the completed poem to him, which he thought poked fun at Thomas's trait of indecisiveness. He hoped the poem might remind Thomas of their walks in England and his difficulty making a decision in those small matters and might help lighten his mood while faced with this larger decision. Thomas did not realize that the poem was intended to be for this purpose, however, until Frost let him know. The British writer did eventually decide to join the fight against the Germans in World War I. When he was killed in action, Frost felt the loss of his friend deeply.

The poem's four stanzas are made up of five lines in each group. The poet uses imagery to depict the two paths in the wood. The speaker looks down the first path in the first stanza and down the next path in the second. In the third stanza he considers them both, and in the last stanza he makes his choice. A close reading of the poem shows that the second path at first appears to be less traveled, but in fact it is worn "really about the same." The poem contains several end rhymes, for example: "wood," "stood," "could," and "both" and "undergrowth." They appear in each stanza in the rhyme scheme or pattern of *abaab*, where the lower case letters represent words that rhyme with each other.

Though in the final stanza, the speaker tells the reader that he chose the path less traveled, in fact, the paths appear to have an equal amount of leaves that "no step had trodden black." He thinks that he may return to go down the first path one day, then thinks better of it, that "way leads on to way," and he will probably never go down that path at all. He chooses the second path.

END RHYME—
Words at the ends of two or more lines that have an exact rhyme.

It is interesting to look closely at the final few lines. Is what has made "all the difference" that the speaker actually chose the less-traveled path, as most readers see the poem, or is it what has made all the difference that the speaker *tells* people "ages and ages hence" that he took the less-traveled path, even though the paths were equally worn?

Either reading makes a fascinating and memorable poem. In fact, in a survey of 18,000 American readers' favorite poems in the year 2000, poet laureate Robert Pinsky discovered that "The Road Not Taken" was mentioned more than any other.

CHAPTER 5

"STOPPING BY WOODS"

A New England Poet, 1920–1924

I n 1920, after his first few years at Amherst College, Frost bought a farm in South Shaftsbury, Vermont, located halfway between Bennington and Arlington. The family called the place "stone house" and farmed apples on the land. They were by now used to moving into old farmhouses that had no running water or indoor plumbing and living that way until these conveniences could be installed. When Frost later moved away, his son Carol adopted this 1779 home with wonderful views of the Vermont landscape as his permanent residence.

JEANIE FROST

About this time as well, Frost heard disturbing stories about his sister, Jeanie. Unfortunately, unlike her brother, Jeanie had not done well after she moved with her mother and brother back to New England after her father's death in California. She was a nervous girl and fought bouts of insomnia and depression throughout school. Occasionally, Frost would stay home during her periods of illness and try to help his mother care for her. Their mother called her "my poor fragile girl."[1]

Jeanie did not apply to any colleges in her senior year of high school. Finally, in December of her senior year she contracted typhoid fever and dropped out of school altogether. After her mother and grandfather died, Jeanie drifted from place to place living on money drawn from her share of her grandfather's annuity. She never really settled into a job or established a lasting adult relationship.

In 1920, Frost learned that his sister had been arrested in Portland, Maine, for disturbing the peace. He had been estranged from her by then for some time and only heard about her through the family's lawyer who was called by the police to come bail her out. The lawyer refused and informed Frost that it was his responsibility to deal with his sister and her problems.

With their parents and grandparents gone, no other siblings to turn to, and four children of his own to raise on an insecure income, Frost chose what may be thought of as the most expedient, if not the most charitable, solution to the problem. He committed his sister to the State Hospital in

The Stone House, where Robert Frost resided from 1920 to 1929.

Augusta, Maine. She died there on September 7, 1929, after living there for nine years, mostly in a state of mental confusion.

BREAD LOAF WRITERS' CONFERENCE

Middlebury College in the Green Mountain area of Vermont founded its Bread Loaf Graduate School of English in 1920. In 1926, the school added a summer program, held in late August before the new fall term began. The Bread Loaf Writers' Conference, as it was called, focused predominantly on writing and the teaching of writing. The concept was that if students and faculty could interact informally outside the walls of the classroom they might be more inspired to create, share ideas, make new discoveries, and experiment more freely with language.

This alternative approach to education attracted Robert Frost. He disliked the regimen of formal classes, lecture halls, and schedules that was the backbone of normal academic life. The setting of the conference in the New England countryside, in an old farmhouse, barn and cottages, and an informal schedule were all that he needed to share his thoughts on poetry with budding poets.

Frost became involved with Bread Loaf early in its history. His first contact with the school was a talk he gave there in 1921 called "The Responsibilities of Teachers of Composition." Frost participated in the Bread Loaf Conference 39 of the next 42 summers, missing visits only in 1922, 1926, and 1932. Each July, he frequently gave a poetry reading in the Little Theatre; he spoke informally with teachers of English quite frequently in the Barn. There are many pictures of Frost sitting outside in the characteristic wooden Adirondack chairs engaged in active conversation with other faculty, writers, and students at the conference.

Frost's notoriety and affiliation with the Bread Loaf Conference helped establish the program at Middlebury and spread this informal method of intense writing instruction across the country. Bread Loaf is the oldest writer's conference in the United States, and was established before there were any formal creative writing programs at colleges. Now, creative writing has become a degree program within English departments of many colleges and universities. The "visiting writer" has become an established position on the faculties of many of these institutions due in large part to the educational philosophy and teaching practices of Robert Frost.

"FIRE AND ICE"

One of the poems from his *New Hampshire* collection that is often anthologized in schoolbooks is the lyric poem "Fire and Ice." The poem originally appeared in *Harper's Magazine* in December 1920. It is one of Frost's shortest poems.

* * *

"FIRE AND ICE"
Some say the world will end in fire,
Some say in ice.
From what I've tasted of desire
I hold with those who favor fire.
But if it had to perish twice,
I think I know enough of hate
To say that for destruction ice
Is also great
And would suffice.

* * *

The poem talks about the end of the world and whether the end will come through fire or through ice. The speaker of the poem links fire with desire and therefore favors, at first, that choice. He would rather that the world be destroyed through wanting too much, trying too hard, through the passion of too much effort on the part of human beings trying to discover, reach, dream. He thinks about destruction through ice, however, which may represent hatred, stillness, and death, and realizes that the world could end just as easily that way. Philosophically and even politically, the poem may be interpreted to suggest that ending the world through passion and love is preferred to inaction and hate. But human nature, the speaker has discovered, is capable of both.

The poem consists of nine lines and is unlike many of Frost's poems in that it does not contain concrete images from the natural world such as apples or stones but instead uses the more abstract imagery of fire and ice that could come in any size, shape, or form. The poem seems fairly simple on the surface, but a study of its *meter* and other sound devices adds complexity.

Several of the lines—1, 3, 4, 5, 6, and 7—contain four iambs (metrical units consisting of a stressed syllable followed by an unstressed syllable) and flow smoothly in iambic meter or rhythmic pattern. Lines 2, 8, and 9 contain only two iambs and disturb the rhythmic flow. Each of those lines is about ice. In addition, the assonance of the poem through the long "i" sound in "fire,"

IAMB—*A metrical unit consisting of a stressed syllable followed by an unstressed syllable.*

ASSONANCE— *Repetition of vowel sounds, for example:* name plain.

"ice," "desire," "twice," "I," and "suffice" echoes the personal pronoun "I" throughout the poem, keeping the focus in a subconscious way on the speaker as the

ALLITERATION—
Repetition of beginning and/or middle consonant sounds, such as little leaf, *or* delicious pudding.

CONSONANCE—
Repetition of ending consonant sounds, for example: fun Manhattan.

common bond between the two elements of fire and water. This promotes the central theme of the poem that the speaker is familiar with both fire and ice. The *alliteration* and *consonance* with the "f" sounds in "fire," "From," "favor," "fire," and "if" link those lines to the fire image. Having no "f" sound in lines 6, 7, and 8 makes the linkage of ice with the "f" sound in "suffice" a strong union between the two images. The concluding word, "suffice," brings to mind a fusion of the words "suffering" and "ice."

The speaker of the poem seems to have discovered that though he would prefer the world to end through the fire that represents desire, he is fully capable of feeling the hatred of ice and believes that that element, too, could also end the world. The poem has been interpreted as a commentary on the "ice" of the Cold War as well; however, the poem was written decades before World War II even began. This is an example of the timelessness of good poetry.

Interpretation: *What might the fire and ice in the poem represent in the world today? What is* your *interpretation of the poem?*

"STOPPING BY WOODS ON A SNOWY EVENING"

The *New Hampshire* collection won the Pulitzer Prize in 1924, and one of its most famous poems, "Stopping by Woods on a Snowy Evening," is perhaps rivaled only by "The Road Not Taken" with the general public as their favorite Robert Frost poem. Young people hear the poem early in school and see it beautifully illustrated in children's anthologies. It is easily memorized, and countless students have recited it in the front of classrooms as part of school assignments.

* * *

"STOPPING BY WOODS ON A SNOWY EVENING"

Whose woods these are I think I know
His house is in the village, though;
He will not see me stopping here
To watch his woods fill up with snow.

My little horse must think it queer
To stop without a farmhouse near
Between the woods and frozen lake
The darkest evening of the year.

He gives his harness bells a shake
To ask if there is some mistake.
The only other sound's the sweep
Of easy wind and downy flake.

The woods are lovely, dark, and deep,
But I have promises to keep,
And miles to go before I sleep,
And miles to go before I sleep.

* * *

The poem is written in four quatrains (a four-line stanza) using a similar rhyme scheme until the last stanza. A particularly fascinating feature of the poem is the interlocking rhyme scheme among the stanzas, meaning that the *b* of the *aaba* rhyme scheme in the first stanza becomes the basis for the rhyme in the second stanza, *bbcb*. Listing schemes for the four stanzas helps readers see visually the way the stanzas interlock with each other aurally through rhyme: *aaba, bbcb, ccdc, dddd*.

QUATRAIN—*A stanza of poetry composed of four lines. It featured a desire to break with traditions and practices of the past and create something new.*

The speaker is traveling by horse and wagon during a snowstorm and makes a momentary stop between a lake and woods to look at and think about the woods he sees. He wonders who may own them. Then the speaker realizes that he knows the owner of the woods has a house in the village and that the owner will not see him stopping to watch his woods fill up with snow.

The imagery of winter in the countryside is beautifully portrayed in the poem. The quiet of the scene is interrupted only by the harness bells the horse shakes as if to ask why they have stopped. The easy wind sweeps and the downy flakes of snow keep falling—the exact rhymes of "sweep" and "keep" and "sleep" provide a sense of harmony within the poem. There is a mysterious attraction to the darkness of these woods for the speaker. He would like to stay and contemplate them some more. Instead, he realizes he has other responsibilities and miles to go in the storm before he will be home safe and sound and asleep in his bed.

The poet uses repetition of the last two lines to emphasize just how many more miles there are to go, as well as to give an emotional impact to the poem. There are many more miles, and the repetition suggests that the speaker feels not only the long distance and difficulty of traveling them on the darkest night of the year but also the time they represent as a period of his life. There is a feeling that the responsibilities he bears when he reaches his destination are heavy, that he might like to put off just a little longer his duty of taking them up again. He longs to be able to stay and think about the woods, but he must keep his promises and move on.

Readers interpret the poem in many ways. It is perhaps an easy poem to apply to one's own life experience. The woods may be a metaphor or symbol for any desire that keeps readers from wanting to honor previous commitments or responsibilities. There is a sense of sadness in the poem, as well, however, as though the woods represent some sort of rest or comfort that being asleep safe and warm at home does not. They are "lovely, dark and deep." Might the woods represent death or beauty, mystery or thought?

> **Interpretation:** *What might the woods represent to the speaker? What do they represent to you if you apply the poem to your life?*

Asked so many times about it in public readings, Frost once described the event in his life that inspired this poem. During the decade when he and his family lived on Derry Farm (1900–1910), he was coming home by horse and wagon from an unsuccessful trip to the market one winter. The weather was poor, and so was his economic status. He realized that he would not be able to purchase any Christmas presents for his children that year. As he was feeling sad on the journey home, the horse suddenly stopped at a bend in the road near the woods.

Frost told a friend it was as though the horse knew right then and there that it needed a good cry and so did he. The poet admitted to crying his heart out in the quiet of the snow until he had no more tears left. Suddenly, the horse gave a quick shake of his harness, and the sound of the bells cheered up the poet enough so he could make it the rest of the way home. Years later, Lesley Frost, the poet's daughter, validated this memory, adding that sometimes a man deserves a good cry and that the snow covered the sound for her father while the horse had instinctively given him the needed time.

Knowing the biographical inspiration of poems, or the story with which poets often answer this common question from audiences, need not change readers' own interpretations of a poem or the feelings they receive from reading it. The poem stands apart from its poet, and readers are free to meet it on their own terms and take their own pleasure from it. "Stopping by Woods on a Snowy Evening" paints a quiet, winter scene that continues to delight new generations of readers year after year.

"THE GIFT OUTRIGHT"

An American Poet, 1924–1963

In 1924, the year he turned fifty, Robert Frost won his first Pulitzer Prize, for his collection of poems called *New Hampshire*. This prestigious award began what would become several decades of national adulation and admiration of Frost as a poet. The New England farmer-poet had become an American artist of the highest order and was awarded the respect and recognition of that honor all across the country. His wrinkled and weathered face, stooped shoulders, and "frosty" and wild white hair symbolized much that Americans liked to believe about themselves. They were a people that embraced Nature and the outdoors, worked hard, and held onto their independence with fierce determination. He would go on to win three other Pulitzer Prizes: in 1930 for *Collected Poems*; in 1937 for *A Further Range*; and in 1943 for *A Witness Tree*.

LOVES AND LOSSES

Despite his growing fame and success, Frost suffered losses in his family that challenged his chronic fight against depression. His daughter Marjorie died in 1934 at age twenty-nine, as a result of complications of childbirth. Elinor was especially devastated by this tragedy.

Elinor herself battled breast cancer and underwent an operation in the fall of 1937. The Frosts had begun to go to Florida for part of the year, and they spent that winter in Gainesville. On their way to their upstairs apartment one day, Elinor collapsed with a severe heart attack. Frost and his son Carol took her into the apartment and called the doctor. The poet grew more and more agitated as the doctor treated his wife through seven more attacks over the course of the next two days. He was so disruptive that the doctor banished him from the bedroom, though he could hear his wife's voice talking with the doctor. At this time, the intonations of her voice in Frost's ears must have taken on special meaning for the poet, who insisted that "the sound of sense" was enough.

Elinor died on March 20, 1938. She and Frost had been married for forty-three years. With the loss of his wife, the poet sunk into a deep depression. He stayed in his room and drew down the shades. A few weeks later, he wrote to a friend about his wife, who had given him just the right balance of companionship and solitude that he needed as a writer: "I shall be all right in public, but I can't tell you how I am going to behave when I am alone. She could always be present to govern my loneliness without making me feel less alone."[1] The poet wrote that he would try to stay active and go out with people, implying that he did not trust his own capacity to handle the loneliness if he stayed home alone for long periods. Beginning with *Twilight*, the special book he had created for the two of them when Elinor was in college, all of his books of poetry up until her death had been dedicated to her.

Over the years, various accounts of the poet's behavior as a husband and father have sometimes been less than favorable. One early biographer suggested that Frost was cold, unkind, or even mean to his wife and children. Reports about discord within the family also suggested that the poet was insensitive toward his loved ones, that he cared more about his work than he did the welfare of his family. Some pointed to the poor example set by his own ruffian father. Others look to Frost's expressions of guilt over moving the family around so much, having so many children, and not having a steady income. Biographers differ in their interpretations of these accounts of the poet's performance as a family man, but more recent scholarship

Robert Frost sits on the floor with his daughter, Leslie, and two of his granddaughters for a game of pick-up sticks in January 1945.

leans toward a sympathetic view. Frost is more often portrayed as a devoted husband who tried to contend with the everyday difficulties of keeping a family of several children afloat on a poet's, and sometimes teacher's, income.

The death of Elinor closed a major phase of the poet's life and opened what some describe as the long final chapter. In June 1938, he wanted to scatter Elinor's ashes along Hyla Brook at Derry Farm, according to her final wishes, but his request was met less than enthusiastically by the owner at the time. Instead, the urn with her ashes was buried in Old Bennington. Unable to stand the loneliness he felt revisiting the places where he and Elinor had lived together, the poet resigned from Amherst College after Elinor's memorial service at Johnson Chapel.

Later in 1938, Frost's emotional distress reached such a depth that some claimed he impulsively asked a family friend, Kathleen "Kay" Morrison, to marry him. There is some mystery and controversy surrounding this supposed "proposal" and whether it actually occurred or if it was clear what the poet was actually trying to do about a possible relationship with Kay. Morrison was already married, as it is said she pointed out to the poet. Instead, she became his assistant, and both she and her husband, Ted Morrison, attempted to provide some company and comfort to the lonely poet through a complex friendship among the three of them. Even so, accounts abound of Frost behaving badly in public on occasion, rebelling against his intense emotions of grief and loneliness by exhibiting quarrelsome and cantankerous moods.

In 1939, Frost was awarded the Ralph Waldo Emerson Fellowship in Poetry at Harvard University, which meant that he was now an official member of the Harvard faculty. Frost taught at the college from 1939-1942. For the rest of his life, he moved from Homer Noble Farm (which he bought in 1939) in Ripton, Vermont, to an apartment in Boston or a duplex in Cambridge, to South Miami, and back again.

On October 9, 1940, the poet suffered another tragic loss. His son Carol had battled the urge to commit suicide for many years. In his father's shadow, Carol had failed at various endeavors—farming, even writing a bit of poetry—and had never been able to find a suitable occupation and focus in life for very long. Carol's son, Prescott, had stayed up late with him that night in 1940, as he talked of suicide again. Prescott knew the situation with his father was not good, and he tried to stay awake to keep him from harming himself.

Finally, fatigue overtook Prescott, the poet's grandson, and he went to bed leaving his father, Carol, alone. When he woke up suddenly from the

Robert Frost is pictured here with his son Carol circa 1915.

sound of a gunshot just after daybreak, he already knew what had happened. He went to the kitchen to find that his father had shot himself in the head with a deer rifle. With a calm and collected manner that the poet later praised him for, Prescott called the police, then his grandfather, then the doctor.

Robert Frost was crushed and looked back thinking over what more he could have done for his son. Though he still held on to his own brand of spiritual beliefs, Frost had long before given up formalized religion and could not cling now to the comfort it offers many people. Instead, he coped the only way he knew how to get through the chaos of life— through the reading and writing of poetry.

POET LAUREATE OF THE UNITED STATES

The poet would spend nearly the last half of his life widely recognized as an elder statesman of American literature and culture. As was his habit when he was younger, he went back and forth between farming, teaching, and writing. Frost became what some might call the unofficial poet laureate of the United States before the designation was made an official post at the Library of Congress in 1937. He served a one-year term in that capacity, in 1958–1959.

Poet Laureate—*Once called Consultant in Poetry to the Library of Congress, the post that developed into the Poet Laureate of the United States is a position where poets are appointed by the Library of Congress to serve the nation. Other poet laureates besides Robert Frost have included Gwendolyn Brooks, Robert Penn Warren, Richard Wilbur, Robert Pinsky, Rita Dove, and Maxine Kumin, among others. It is the task of the poet laureate to promote the reading and appreciation of poetry around the country. Laureates have the freedom to do this in ways of their own choosing that they find most effective. More recent laureates have actively pursued programs to bring poetry to the people and encourage poetry writing.*

It did not go unnoticed in Frost's time that he was born two years before the first centennial of the country. He was held in esteem and affection by most readers around the world as an American treasure. He once said that he hoped to live to be 100 years old because, if he did, he would have lived through half of the country's history. He almost made it.

A POET ABROAD

Despite his preference for New England and his dread of flying, as Frost became more and more successful and an American icon at home and abroad, he was coaxed to make several international trips as a cultural ambassador. In August 1954, he attended the World Congress of Writers in São Paulo, Brazil. He and writer William Faulkner were the official representatives at the request of the U.S. State Department.

In 1957, he was asked by Sherman Adams, former New Hampshire governor and then-assistant to President Eisenhower, to go to England. His mission was to remind the British of their cultural ties and fellowship with the United States. While in England and Ireland, he received honorary degrees from several universities, including both Oxford and Cambridge. Frost was the first American writer since Henry Wadsworth Longfellow in 1868 and James Russell Lowell in 1873 to receive these prestigious recognitions.

While in England, when he was more than eighty years old, Frost was expected to go to meetings, give readings and lectures, and participate in press conferences. In the middle of his busy schedule, Frost was able to revisit the Gloucestershire/Herefordshire countryside where he had worked on his first two books of poems four decades earlier. He even stopped at Little Iddens, the cottage he and his family rented in 1914.

In 1961, Frost went to Israel as the first Samuel Paley Lecturer at Hebrew University. While there, he was moved by and commented on the rocky elements of the city of Jerusalem, of seeing one stone wall after another erected by earlier civilizations.

Robert Frost on his eighty-fifth birthday in 1959.

Seeing firsthand the sites of the Bible, it struck the poet that the area was a solid connection between ancient times and his own. He said that no other event he ever participated in made him feel his own connection to antiquity as much as that visit.

JOHN F. KENNEDY'S INAUGURATION

The presidential election of 1960 was a close one. Candidate Richard Nixon was narrowly defeated by Massachusetts senator John F. Kennedy. Frost pledged his support so strongly for fellow New Englander Kennedy that it was almost as though he carried on a quiet campaign for the senator. Kennedy was an author himself and liked poetry. He often quoted the last line of "Stopping by Woods on a Snowy Evening" at the close of his speeches, speaking about having miles to go before he slept.

Arizona congressman Stewart L. Udall knew Frost and suggested to Kennedy that he might consider inviting Frost to read poetry at the inauguration. At first Kennedy objected, joking that the poet always stole the show at any performance of which he was a part. Finally, though, he agreed that including this respected elder in the ceremony would help set the tone for his new administration.

Kennedy called Frost in Cambridge and spoke with him about possible poems that he might read. At first, Kennedy requested that Frost write a new poem for the occasion. Frost bristled at this suggestion saying that it could not be done. Poets do not write poems made to order. Considering alternatives, Kennedy suggested "The Gift Outright," with the special request that Frost change one line to read more optimistically, changing "would" to "will" in the last line. Frost indicated that he would think about it. Poets of Frost's stature in general do not like to touch even a single word of a completed poem at another person's request. To a poet, this would be something like changing the hair color in a portrait simply because the viewer preferred blondes. It is simply not done—it would affect the integrity of the art as well as the artist.

In the end, Frost did attempt to write a new poem for the special day in Washington, D.C. As it turned out, the hurried lines became a preamble to "The Gift Outright." He called this introductory statement "For John F. Kennedy His Inauguration." The verses of the preamble were not as successful as the poem itself. The lines were typed in the hotel office the night before the inauguration, and the print was very light. The lines were retyped in the morning in larger type with fresh ink.

The ceremony was to begin at ten o'clock on a bright, sunny, and very cold morning on January 20, 1961. Snow covered the ground, and the huge audience at the U.S. Capitol, as well as the millions of citizens in their homes watching on their black-and-white televisions all across the country, could see the puffs of the participants' breath in the cold air. Richard Cardinal Cushing gave the invocation and Marian Anderson sang the national anthem. The new vice-president, Lyndon B. Johnson, was sworn in. Robert Frost was summoned to take his turn and the octogenarian walked slowly to the podium.

The sunlight fell on his white papers so brightly that he could not read the words because of the glare. The old man standing there in his black topcoat, his white hair sticking out every which way, announced that he was having trouble reading, and people wondered if he could pull this moment off.

Vice-President Johnson tried to shield the sun for the poet with his top hat, but Frost waved him off. Finally, Frost gathered his characteristic feisty strength and saved the situation. Rather than bother with trying to read the new preamble, which may have even struck him by this time as somewhat artificial, he moved directly into a sound and firm recitation by heart of "The Gift Outright." These were the more genuine lines of his presentation in any case. The

Robert Frost, along with his children and grandchildren, are entertained by folk singer Danny Gragon, playing the fiddle.

crowd was delighted. As Kennedy had requested, the poet concluded the poem triumphantly, "Such as she was, such as she *would* become, *has* become, and I— and for this occasion let me change that to—what she *will* become."[2]

"THE GIFT OUTRIGHT"

The poem Frost recited at President Kennedy's inauguration was written as early as 1935 and first appeared in print in the *Virginia Quarterly Review* in 1942. It was then printed as part of the collection *A Witness Tree* later the same year. Frost first read the poem in public at William and Mary College.

* * *

"THE GIFT OUTRIGHT"

The land was ours before we were the land's.
She was our land more than a hundred years
Before we were her people. She was ours
In Massachusetts, in Virginia,
But we were England's, still colonials,
Possessing what we still were unpossessed by,
Possessed by what we now no more possessed.
Something we were withholding made us weak
Until we found out that it was ourselves
We were withholding from our land of living,
And forthwith found salvation in surrender.
Such as we were we gave ourselves outright
(The deed of gift was many deeds of war)

To the land vaguely realizing westward,
But still unstoried, artless, unenhanced,
Such as she was, such as she would become.

* * *

In some ways, the poem sounds dated to twenty-first-century ears. The speaker talks about the land of the United States and how its people were owned by it before they moved westward and came to own the land through a strange kind of surrender to its mysteries. There is no mention of Native Americans in the poem, only the presence of the Old World of Europe in contrast with the New World colonies of Massachusetts and Virginia. The "unstoried" land in the speaker's view was, in fact, many storied with religious narratives, myths, and legends of the first people who already lived there long before European colonization.

The "many deeds of war" appear to glorify the American Revolution as well as some of the uglier moments of the country's history during the Westward expansion when European immigrants moved across the continent through Indian lands. A suggestion of Frost's acknowledgement of this occurs, however, in the "vaguely realizing westward" phrase in line 14.

Interest in the poem comes from considering the play on words, with gift-giving likened to a deed that

Robert Frost peers out the window of the cottage of fellow poet Wilfrid Gibson on June 1, 1957.

must be performed in order to obtain the deed to the land. According to this interpretation, by surrendering ourselves to the land, the people of the United States have gained their identity as a nation. Among critics and scholars, this poem has not been so much praised for its artistry as a sixteen-line sonnet but rather for the historical significance of being read at John F. Kennedy's inauguration.

MEETING NIKITA KHRUSHCHEV

In May 1962, while in Washington, D.C., meeting Stewart Udall and Anatoly Dobrynin, the Soviet Ambassador to the United States, Frost was asked whether he might be interested in visiting the Soviet Union on a cultural exchange. He indicated interest but also made it clear that he would only go as an official representative if the request came from the president himself. And if he were to go, he wanted to meet Premier Nikita Khrushchev. Soon after, President Kennedy did formally ask the eighty-eight year-old Frost, who had just recovered not long before from a bout of pneumonia, if he might go to the Soviet Union as his emissary to help warm relations between the two countries. It was the height of the Cold War, and, as it turned out, just weeks before the standoff that would become the Cuban Missile Crisis.

The **Cold War** was the four-decade-long period, from the end of World War II until the fall of the Berlin Wall in 1989, of ideological tensions among countries around the world. Principally, the conflict between Communist countries and "the West" arose because stockpiles of nuclear and other weapons threatened mass destruction and both sides mistrusted each other's motives. The struggle was symbolized by relations between the two superpowers of the world during the era—the Soviet Union and the United States.

The **Cuban Missile Crisis** was a key event of the Cold War that occurred in October 1962. American intelligence reported that the Soviet Union had placed long-range missiles on the island of Cuba, just miles away from the Florida Keys, and aimed them in the direction of Washington, D.C. President John F. Kennedy issued an ultimatum to the Soviet Union, ordering Premier Nikita Khrushchev to remove the missiles immediately or risk military retaliation. If Khrushchev refused to remove the missiles, there was a real risk that the two countries might be on the verge of nuclear war. Over the course of just a few hours, Washington held its collective breath, waiting to learn Khrushchev's response. In the end, the Soviet Union agreed to remove the weapons and the crisis abated.

"How grand for you to think of me this way and how like you to take the chance of sending anyone like me over there affinitizing with the Russians," Frost replied in a letter to the president. "I shall be reading poems chiefly, over there, but I shall be talking some where I read and you may be sure I won't be talking just literature."[3] The poet was excited to be invited on such an important mission by the president. He was concerned chiefly about his health and physical condition.

That problem was eased by having a friend, Frederick B. Adams, director of the Pierpont Morgan Library in New York, accompany him. Stewart Udall, by then U.S. Secretary of the Interior, went as head of the delegation. F.D. Reeve, a young poet and Russian translator, also went along.

Frost arrived in the Soviet Union on August 29, 1962. One of the events planned was a public reading at Pushkin House, in Leningrad (now, St. Petersburg). The place was packed, and the elder poet recited several of his poems, including "Birches" and "Mending Wall." The Russians, who are great fans of literature, and poetry in particular, gave Frost an enthusiastic ovation.

Though he was having a good trip, it was Frost's personal mission to meet Premier Nikita Khrushchev. Even in very old age, there was a feistiness still remaining in Frost from the scrappy days of his youth that made him want to look power in the face and show that he would not flinch. The meeting began to look doubtful when Udall went ahead of Frost to the Soviet republic of Georgia, where Khrushchev was

Robert Frost enjoys casual conversation among friends in November 1958.

staying. Frost was outraged, thinking he had been left behind in Moscow. Instead, he was invited to join them a bit later.

During this trip, however, Frost suffered from painful stomach cramps. He refused to stay in Moscow when advised to do so. When they reached Georgia, Frost was taken to the Ministry of Health for rest and food. There, he was examined by a local doctor. She told him that he perhaps suffered from nervous indigestion and recommended returning to Moscow for more tests. Frost refused. He had come all this way to meet Khrushchev on behalf of the president, and he would not be deterred.

As he was resting, Frost was informed that Khrushchev was sending his personal physician to look after him and that he would drop by himself to visit him at the guest house where he was staying. The doctor arrived, examined the American poet, and recommended a bland diet and bed rest. Not long afterward, Frost was told that Khrushchev himself had arrived at the guest house. Frost, nervous but eager to see him, rose out of bed to put on his socks and shoes before the premier entered his room.

Khrushchev walked in wearing an olive-tan suit and beige Ukrainian shirt, which was less formal clothing than Americans were used to seeing him in on their television screens. Their meeting would last ninety minutes, much longer than anyone anticipated. Their conversation ranged over topics from greetings from President Kennedy to poetry to politics.

According to Jay Parini in *Robert Frost: A Life*, Khrushchev was friendly and polite with the poet. After a time, however, he sensed that Frost really had something specific on his mind, and when he questioned him about it, Frost expressed his opinion that East and West Berlin should unify. He offered his reasons on foreign policy grounds, and Khrushchev discussed with him why this was impossible from the Soviet Union's point of view.

Toward the end of their meeting, Khrushchev asked Frost if he might be getting tired, but Frost said that he was feeling much better. The premier said that it had been a pleasure for him to meet such an eminent poet, and he asked that Frost take his greetings back to President Kennedy with him. As the premier was about to leave the guest house grounds, Reeve reminded Frost that he had wanted to give the leader a signed copy of his book, *In the Clearing*, so the poet gave the book to Reeve to run out to Khrushchev.

Frost was elated with the meeting. He was greatly impressed with Khrushchev. He commented right after the meeting to Reeve, "He's a great man. He knows what power is and isn't afraid to take hold of it. He's a great man all right."[4] Frost had supported Kennedy for president, but he believed that power must be deterred with power, and his meeting with the Soviet premier only strengthened his opinion.

Unfortunately, Frost was exhausted when he returned to the United States on a seventeen-hour flight on September 9, 1962. The press was there to greet him when he descended the Pam American jet at Idlewild Airport in New York. "Khrushchev said we were too liberal to fight," he commented offhandedly to the reporters.[5] When asked if he brought back a message from the premier to President Kennedy, he replied that he did, but that he would wait for the president to contact him before he would deliver it.

President Kennedy did not ask to meet with Frost after his return from the Soviet Union. Many interpreted the dismissal as a response to Frost's offhand remarks at the airport. It was believed that the Kennedy administration did not appreciate Frost's public repetition of Khrushchev's opinion that the Americans would not stand and fight if push came to shove. Frost maintained his view that power only understood and respected a competing power rather than diplomacy alone. This doctrine would later be adopted by President Ronald Reagan in his dealings with the Russians two decades later. Because it appeared to affect his relationship with the

Robert Frost recites some of his poetry for students and faculty at Amherst in May 1959.

president, however, Frost regretted making his weary comment in the airport interview.

THE DARKER SIDE OF FROST

Though Robert Frost is regarded as a great American poet, and his place in literature is secure, readers of his biography are sometimes reminded that he was a living, breathing human being with good and bad characteristics just like everyone else. President John F. Kennedy said at the dedication of the Frost Library at Amherst College, "If Robert Frost was much honored in his lifetime, it was because a good many preferred to ignore his darker truths."[6] During the summer of 1938 at Bread Loaf, Frost and one of his poet friends, Bernard DeVoto, had a disagreement. When they left the conference, DeVoto said to Frost, "You're a good poet, Robert, but you're a bad man."[7]

People who knew Frost, such as biographer Lawrance Thompson, sometimes described a man who was arrogant, quarrelsome, stubborn, cantankerous, and set in his ways. For his part, Thompson had spent a good deal of time with the poet, enough so that bad feelings and misunderstandings grew between them over several issues. Later critics and biographers claimed that Thompson had become too close to the story he was trying to tell, and this affected his objectivity. His multivolume biography of the poet tended to emphasize Frost's faults and went a long way to set up the initial negative mythology surrounding the man.

Sometimes Frost behaved in public as though he wanted to perpetuate the emphasis on his troublesome traits. At times the poet was reported to have spoken insensitively about various groups, such as women and Jews. Those who support Frost argue that it is unfair to impose twenty-first-century sensibilities on a man who was born, after all, less than a decade after the Civil War. They suggest that some of the criticism of his speech and behavior ignores Frost's portrayal of these groups in his writing or teaching. Supporters argue, for example, that the female persona, Mary, in "The Death of the Hired Man," is described realistically, positively, and with insight. They point out that Frost not only taught in Israel, but loved the Old Testament, and was a close associate of prominent Jews such as Louis Untermeyer and Rabbi Weichert. Whether it contributes positively or negatively to one's interpretation of a person's character, speech, and actions, historical and cultural context are important factors to consider. Context does not excuse insensitivity in some readers' minds, but it may help explain or clarify where unacceptable attitudes may have come from or how genuine, deep, or mean-spirited they really were.

A demon the poet fought in his personal life was his family's tendency toward depression. He feared slipping into his institutionalized sister's fate if he were not careful. Often he doubted whether he measured up to the kind of poet he wanted to be. Even his most-devoted fans admit that not all of his published poetry is top quality. Often the poet's feelings of self-doubt played themselves out on his family. Some accounts claim that, like his father before him, he could be physically rough with family members. Suicide crossed his mind on more than one occasion, and he was devastated when his own son Carol took his life on October 9, 1940.

A successful poet must come to grips with the dark times of life as much as with the awards, accolades, and successes of being a recognized artist. That Robert Frost lived eighty-eight years and achieved such success shows that he managed to find a way to walk in and around life's tangled obstacles and survive.

DEEPER INTO LIFE

On January 27, 1963, the poet Ezra Pound's daughter, Princess Mary de Rachewiltz, came by Boston's Peter Bent Brigham Hospital to thank Frost for his efforts on her father's behalf. Pound, the poet who

Frost is greeted by President Kennedy and his wife, Jackie, during a party given for Nobel prize winners at the White House in 1962.

had favorably reviewed Frost's early work, had been imprisoned as a traitor for broadcasting anti-American propaganda in Italy during World War II. Frost had supported his incarceration, but later publicly supported Archibald MacLeish's efforts to have Pound institutionalized at St. Elizabeth's Hospital in Washington, D.C., when it became obvious that the poet was too ill to stand trial.

After Pound's daughter left, Frost dictated a letter thanking friends for wishing him a swift recovery from his surgery for prostate cancer and multiple complications. In the letter, he said, "If only I get well . . . I'll go deeper into my life."[8] Unfortunately, the complications continued, and Frost mentioned to another friend that afternoon that he felt like he might be within hours of death. He died near midnight the next day, on January 29, 1963, from a pulmonary embolism, a blood clot that reached his lungs.

Frost once said that all he hoped to ever accomplish in life as a poet was to "lodge a few poems where they couldn't be gotten rid of easily."[9] By all accounts, the eighty-eight year-old poet achieved his goal.

FROST'S LEGACY

Frost lived long enough to be honored in his own time with dozens of prizes and honorary degrees. He received the Congressional Gold Medal in 1962. After he received the medal at the White House from President Kennedy, Frost requested that the medal be kept at the Houghton Library at Harvard University in memory of his father's experience at the school as well as his own years there as a student and a teacher.

On his eighty-fifth birthday, he was thrown an elaborate party at New York's Waldorf-Astoria with literary giants such as Lionel Trilling and W.H. Auden in attendance. Louis Untermeyer, Frost's longtime friend, and to whom he had written more than two hundred letters over nearly fifty years, was also there. Untermeyer would later publish the correspondence in a book called *The Letters of Robert Frost to Louis Untermeyer*. The book became a gift to later students and scholars of Frost, especially because of what the letters reveal of Frost's ideas about poetry and about his biography through the decades. Frost's appearances, teaching, recordings of his poems, and other public performances provided a trail of people who knew him, heard him speak, or recorded his words. Future biographers, students, and scholars used their reminiscences to learn more about the man and his work. Decades after his death, there are still people alive who remember the poet in the flesh and have a Robert Frost story they can tell.

Robert Frost receives the Congressional Gold Medal from President Kennedy on March 26, 1962.

In American literature, Robert Frost's contribution remains important in form and subject matter. By placing the voice of the common New Englander into traditional poetic forms, the method he called "sound of sense," Frost achieved an art that could at once be appreciated by the everyday reader at the same time that its complexities made it endure the test of time and study by academics, literary critics, and scholars. Though Frost wrote with an eye toward the ancient Greek and Latin classics he studied as a young man, clarity was key.

The Poetry of Robert Frost: The Collected Poems, edited by Edward Connery Lathem, who knew Frost, brings together poems from the poet's nine individual collections over nearly five decades. The book contains more than 350 poems. Frost's poetry not only affected readers but it also influenced poets and writers who came after him such as Theodore Roethke, Donald Hall, Maxine Kumin, Seamus Heaney, Galway Kinnell, Richard Wilbur, Wendell Berry, and others.

The world came to know America through the introduction to its New England countryside and way of life on a more personal, intimate level. Though the imagery of his poetry is specific to a certain region of the world, the appeal of its subject matter and themes is universal. There are rural

Robert Frost is shown here at age eighty-seven.

regions in every country on earth, though their climates and terrains may differ. Even in the age of high technology, people in the United States and elsewhere continue to work the land with their hands, use tools, or talk with their neighbors about the fences of all kinds that exist between them. The poet once said, "I talk about the whole world in terms of New England."[10]

Frost is less known for his writing in other areas, such as his prose and drama. However, he did write speeches and published plays *A Way Out, The Guardeen,* and *In an Art Factory.* Two other "closet dramas," *A Masque of Reason* and *A Masque of Mercy* were produced for the stage.

Frost's contributions to education from his years of teaching at primary school through college are also not as well known but are important nonetheless. These include the idea of the artist-in-residence in high schools, colleges, and universities; endowed chairs in high schools (specially funded faculty positions); and the teaching of American literature, as opposed to British literature exclusively, as had been the tradition. He and Elinor were also among the early proponents of a new generation of homeschooling after public education became the norm.

As a cultural icon for much of the twentieth-century, Robert Frost helped promote American poetry and culture around the world at a time when the United States became one of the two major superpowers militarily and economically. As President Kennedy said, "Robert Frost was one of the granite figures in our time in America. He was supremely two things: an artist and an American."[11]

CHRONOLOGY

1874—On March 26, Robert Frost is born in San Francisco, California, to Isabelle (Belle) Moodie and William Prescott Frost, Jr. He is named after the Confederate general, Robert E. Lee, whom his father admired.

1876—On June 25, Jeanie Florence Frost, Robert Frost's sister, is born in the grandparents' home in Lawrence, Massachusetts. When Robert, his mother, and new sister return to San Francisco in November, his alcoholic father is diagnosed with consumption (tuberculosis).

1885—On May 5, William Frost dies of tuberculosis, leaving the family only $8.00 after funeral expenses. The family moves in with Robert's paternal grandparents in Lawrence, Massachusetts. They also spend time in Amherst, New Hampshire, at the farm of Robert's great-aunt, Sarah Frost.

1886—The Frost family moves to Salem Depot, New Hampshire, where Robert's mother begins teaching fifth to eighth grades in the school district.

1889—Robert completes the school year in Massachusetts at Lawrence High School at the head of his class. Older friend Carl Burell introduces him to astronomy, botany, and the theory of evolution.

1890—In April Robert publishes his first poem, "La Noche Triste," in the Lawrence High School *Bulletin*.

1892—Frost graduates from Lawrence High School as co-valedictorian with Elinor White, and delivers the commencement speech, "A Monument to After-Thought Unveiled." He enters Dartmouth College but leaves before the semester is out.

1894—Frost publishes "My Butterfly: An Elegy," which he regarded as his first poem, in the November 8 issue of *The Independent*. He privately publishes two copies of *Twilight* in an attempt to woo Elinor White.

1895—On December 19, Frost marries Elinor White and works as a journalist.

1896—On September 25, son, Elliott, is born.

1897—Frost enrolls as a freshman at Harvard.

1899—On March 31, Frost withdraws from Harvard out of concern over his and his family's health. On April 28, daughter, Lesley, is born.

1900—Elliott dies of cholera on July 8. The family moves to maternal grandfather's farm at Derry, New Hampshire. Robert Frost's mother, Belle, dies on November 2.

1902—On May 27, son, Carol, is born.

1903—On June 27, daughter, Irma, is born.

1905—On March 28, daughter, Marjorie, is born.

1906—Frost takes a teaching position at Pinkerton Academy, in Derry, New Hampshire.

1907—Daughter, Elinor Bettina, is born on June 18 and dies on June 21.

1909—Frost publishes "Into My Own" in *New England Magazine*. The family leaves the farm and moves to Derry Village.

1911—The Frost family moves to Plymouth, New Hampshire, where Frost teaches at Plymouth Normal School. The Derry farm is sold.

1912—The Frost family moves to England and rents a cottage in Beaconsfield, Buckinghamshire, 20 miles north of London. Frost collects and revises poems for *A Boy's Will*.

1913—*A Boy's Will* is published in April in England. Frost meets the poet Ezra Pound.

1914—The Frost family moves to Dymock, Gloucestershire. *North of Boston* is published in May. Frost learns that the American publisher Henry Holt will publish his books in the United States; he decides to return to the country.

1915—*North of Boston* is published in the U.S. Frost buys a farm in Franconia, New Hampshire; he befriends Louis Untermeyer.

1916—*Mountain Inverval* is published. Frost takes a teaching position at Amherst College in Amherst, Massachusetts.

1920—Frost leaves Amherst College; institutionalizes sister, Jeanie. Moves to Stone House, Vermont, to farm apples. Begins association with Bread Loaf School Writers' Conference at Middlebury College.

1921—Frost takes a one-year fellowship in letters at the University of Michigan.

1923—*Selected Poems* is published in March. Frost returns to Amherst College. *New Hampshire* is published in November. Son Carol marries.

1924—Frost wins Pulitzer Prize for *New Hampshire*. First grandchild, William Prescott Frost, is born to son Carol and his wife, Lillian.

1928—*West-Running Brook* is published. Frost visits France, England, Scotland, and Ireland. Sees Yeats and meets T.S. Eliot.

1930—*Collected Poems* is published in November.

1931—Frost wins Pulitzer Prize for *Collected Poems*.

1936—*A Further Range* is published in May.

1937—Frost receives Pulitzer Prize for *A Further Range*.

1938—Elinor Frost dies on March 20. Kathleen Morrison becomes Frost's companion and assistant.

1939—Expanded *Collected Poems* is published. Frost buys Homer Noble Farm in Ripton, Vermont.

1940—Son Carol dies by suicide on October 9.

1941—Frost summers in Ripton and winters in South Miami.

1942—*A Witness Tree* is published in April.

1943—Frost receives Pulitzer Prize for *A Witness Tree*.

1945—*A Masque of Reason* is published in March.

1947—*Steeple Bush* is published in May.

1949—*Complete Poems of Robert Frost 1949* is published.

1957—Frost travels to England and Ireland and receives honors.

1961—Reads "A Gift Outright" at John F. Kennedy's inauguration. Becomes emissary for State Department and travels to Israel and Greece.

1962—Frost is hospitalized in South Miami with pneumonia. *In the Clearing* is published. Visits the Soviet Union and meets Premier Nikita Khrushchev as State Department emissary. Receives Congressional Gold Medal.

1963—Frost is awarded the Bollingen Prize for Poetry on January 3. Dies January 29 from a pulmonary embolism. Frost's ashes are buried at Old Bennington Cemetery, Old Bennington, Vermont.

Chapter Notes

Chapter 1. From Farmer Poet to Poet Laureate

1. Tyler B. Hoffman, "Poetic Theories," *The Robert Frost Encyclopedia*, eds. Nancy Lewis Tuten and John Zubizarreta (Westport, Conn.: Greenwood Press, 2000), p. 280.

2. Robert Frost, *Selected Letters of Robert Frost*, ed. Lawrance Thompson (New York: Holt, Rinehart, and Winston, 1964), p. 361.

3. Robert Frost, *Complete Poems*, 1949 (New York: Holt, 1949), p. vi.

Chapter 2. A Swinger of Birches

1. "Dartmouth: A Brief History," n.d., <http://www.dartmouth.edu/home/about/history.html> (November 13, 2004).

2. Robert Frost, *Selected Letters of Robert Frost*, ed. Lawrance Thompson (New York: Holt, Rinehart, and Winston, 1964), p. 167.

3. Jay Parini, *Robert Frost: A Life* (New York: Henry Holt and Company, 1999), p. 35.

4. Ibid.

5. F. Brett Cox, "Palgrave's *Golden Treasury*," *The Robert Frost Encyclopedia*, eds. Nancy Lewis Tuten and

John Zubizarreta (Westport, Conn.: Greenwood Press, 2000), p. 263.

6. Lea Newman, *Robert Frost: The People, Places, and Stories Behind his New England Poetry* (Shelburne, Vt.: New England Press, 2000), p. 3.

7. Frost, *Selected Letters*, p. 552.

CHAPTER 3. "MENDING WALL"

1. Paola Loreto, "Ralph Waldo Emerson," *The Robert Frost Encyclopedia*, eds. Nancy Lewis Tuten and John Zubizarreta (Westport, Conn.: Greenwood Press, 2000), p. 93.

2. Ralph Waldo Emerson, "Experience," in *Emerson's Prose and Poetry*, Norton Critical Edition, eds. Joel Porte and Saundra Morris (New York: W. W. Norton, 2001), pp. 198 and 209.

3. Lea Newman, *Robert Frost: The People, Places, and Stories Behind his New England Poetry* (Shelburne, Vt.: New England Press, 2000), p. 73.

4. Ralph Waldo Emerson, "Nature," from *Essays: Second Series* (1844), n.d., <http://www.vcu.edu/eng-web/transcendentalism/authors/emerson/essays/nature1844.html#crit> (November 14, 2004).

5. Ralph Waldo Emerson, "Fate," in *Emerson's Prose and Poetry*, p. 274.

CHAPTER 4. "THE ROAD NOT TAKEN"

1. William Shakespeare, *Macbeth*, Act V, Scene V,

lines 28-33 <http://www.bartleby.com/70/4155.html> (November 15, 2004).

CHAPTER 5. "STOPPING BY WOODS"

1. Jay Parini, *Robert Frost: A Life* (New York: Henry Holt and Company, 1999), p. 28.

CHAPTER 6. "THE GIFT OUTRIGHT"

1. Robert Frost, *Selected Letters of Robert Frost*, ed. Lawrance Thompson (New York: Holt, Rinehart, and Winston, 1964), p. 470.

2. Jay Parini, *Robert Frost: A Life* (New York: Henry Holt and Company, 1999), p. 414.

3. Frost, *Selected Letters*, p. 589.

4. Parini, p. 434.

5. Edward Connery Lathem, ed., *Interviews with Robert Frost* (New York: Holt, Rinehart, and Winston, 1966), p. 291.

6. John F. Kennedy, "Remarks at Amherst College," October 23, 1964, <http://www.jfklibrary.org/j102663.htm> (November 11, 2004).

7. Frost, *Selected Letters*, p. 481.

8. Ibid., p. 596.

9. Jay Parini, "The Art of Reading Robert Frost: A Biographer's Confession," *Poets & Writers Magazine*, n.d., <http://www.pw.org/mag/parini.htm> (November 16, 2004).

10. Helen Bacon, "Frost and the Ancient Muses,"

The Cambridge Companion to Robert Frost, ed. Robert Faggen (Cambridge, England: Cambridge University Press, 2001), p. 75.

11. John F. Kennedy, "Remarks at Amherst College," October 23, 1964, <http://www.jfklibrary.org/j102663.htm> (November 11, 2004).

GLOSSARY

alliteration—Repetition of beginning and/or middle consonant sounds, such as *little leaf*, or *delicious pudding*.

allusion—A direct or indirect reference in a literary work to details from another literary work, mythology, history, or some other source.

assonance—Repetition of vowel sounds, for example: *name plain*.

consonance—Repetition of ending consonant sounds, for example: *fun Manhattan*.

dramatic monologue—A kind of poetic strategy in which the speaker tells the poem to a listener (the auditor) inside the poem.

dramatic poem—Verse that tells a story through action and dialogue, as though it were a miniature play.

end rhyme—Words at the ends of two or more lines that have an exact rhyme.

exact rhyme—When two or more words end with the same vowel and consonant sounds. It is the traditional rhyme most people think of, for example: *wall* and *ball*.

explicate—To explain each line of a poem in your own words.

free verse—Poetry that does not follow a traditional fixed form. Instead, the poet allows the form of the poem to rise "organically" out of the subject matter of the poem.

iamb—A metrical unit consisting of a stressed syllable followed by an unstressed syllable.

imagery—Words or phrases that engage one or more of the five senses—sight, touch, hearing, smell, or taste, for example: *swinging birches*, or *warm sun*.

intonation—The natural rise and fall in pitch of human voices engaged in informal speech.

line breaks—Where the poet chooses to stop a line of verse and begin a new line.

metaphor—A comparison between two seemingly unlike things without using the words "like" or "as," for example: *All the world is a stage.*

meter—A regular pattern of stressed and unstressed syllables in poetry.

modernism—A movement in literature and art that began in the early twentieth century. It featured a desire to break with traditions and practices of the past and create something new.

pastoral poetry—Verses that express a longing for rural life and simplicity of thought and feeling.

personae—Characters in a poem.

personification—A poetic device in which inanimate objects and animals are given human characteristics, for example: *The flower sipped the raindrops.*

poetic device—Any one of numerous techniques of using language in creating poetry, for example: repetition, line breaks, alliteration, assonance, rhyme, and so forth.

poetic forms—Pre-established patterns of numbers of lines and metrical patterns, also called fixed form poetry, that have evolved through poetic tradition over time. Examples of poetic forms are the sonnet, villanelle, and haiku. The poet writing in a fixed form writes to fit the form.

quatrain—A stanza of poetry composed of four lines.

rhyme scheme—A pattern using lower case letters to illustrate which lines of a poem rhyme. Example: When the first and third lines rhyme and the second and fourth lines rhyme, the scheme is illustrated as *abab*.

rhythm—A regular pattern of meter.

sentimentality—In literature, overdramatizing emotions beyond what really happens in an attempt to draw an emotional response from the reader.

simile—A comparison between two seemingly unlike things using the words "like" or "as," for example: *My love is **like** a red, red rose.*

speaker—The narrator of a poem.

stanza—A grouping of poetic lines separated by a space.

tone—The poet's attitude toward the subject as reflected in the writing; the mood of the poem.

Major Works by Robert Frost

Poetry Collections

A Boy's Will (London: Nutt, 1913)
North of Boston (London: Nutt, 1914)
Mountain Interval (New York: Holt, 1916)
New Hampshire (New York: Holt, 1923)
West-Running Brook (New York: Holt, 1928)
Collected Poems (New York: Holt, 1930)
A Further Range (New York: Holt, 1936)
Collected Poems, 2nd edition (New York: Holt, 1939)
A Witness Tree (New York: Holt, 1942)
Steeple Bush (New York: Holt, 1947)
In the Clearing (New York: Holt, 1962)

Verse Plays:

A Masque of Reason (New York: Holt, 1945)
A Masque of Mercy (New York: Holt, 1947)

FURTHER READING

Bloom, Harold, ed. *Robert Frost*. Broomall, Pa.: Chelsea House, 2002.

Faggen, Robert. *The Cambridge Companion to Robert Frost*. Cambridge, England: Cambridge University Press, 2001.

Newman, Lea. *Robert Frost: The People, Places, and Stories Behind his New England Poetry*. Shelburne, Vt.: New England Press, 2000.

Tuten, Nancy Lewis and John Zubizarreta, editors. *The Robert Frost Encyclopedia*. Westport, Conn.: Greenwood Press, 2000.

Audio Recording:

Frost, Robert. *Voice of the Poet*. Caedmon, 2003.

INTERNET ADDRESSES

The Friends of Robert Frost
http://www.frostfriends.org

The Robert Frost Society
http://www.robertfrostsociety.org/

The Robert Frost Foundation
http://www.frostfoundation.org/

INDEX